Mourning rites in
the Pharaonic period

Hair and Death in Ancient Egypt

María Rosa Valdesogo

BLKVLD

BLKVLD Uitgevers Publishers

Book design and cover design - Lonneke Beukenholdt

ISBN 9789492940087

Content

Foreword

This research was started when Dr. Nadine Guilhou from the university of Montpellier told me about some images in Egyptian iconography where hair in funerary rites was treated in a very special way.

The first important document was a vignette in the chapter 168 of the *Book of the Dead* belonging to Muthetepti and dating from the III Intermediate Period. Here the mourning women in the cortege of Re were shaking their hair and covering their faces with it.

For being sure that it was not an isolated case we tried to find out more similar examples. In many tombs from the New Kingdom mourning women gesticulated in the same way; in Thebes the tombs of Amenemhat (TT82), Minakht (TT87), Rekhmire (TT100) and Ineni (TT81), or the tomb of Renni in el-Kab were the most evident examples that it was a common practice in funerals of Ancient Egypt. Out of the burials, but always in the funerary context, there is also a scene from the funerary temple of Seti I in Dra Abu el-Naga, where the two mourners stand at both ends of the corpse shaking their manes of hair.

Such a common attitude could not be just a coincidence, or a theatrical exposure of pain, but it had to arise from a deeper reason related to the funeral rite. The importance of hair in mortuary context seemed to be real, since funerary texts also mentioned it constantly. So, we had to search about its role in both symbolic and ceremonial spheres.

The *Coffin Texts* from the Middle Kingdom were the chosen manuscript as starting point, due to the big amount of allusions to the hair; therefore the *Pyramid Texts* from the Old Kingdom and the *Book of the Dead* from the New Kingdom were considered more as support documents.

Summing up, funerary texts and iconography have been the main sources in this research about the hair in the funerary belief of Ancient Egypt.

2019,
María Rosa Valdesogo

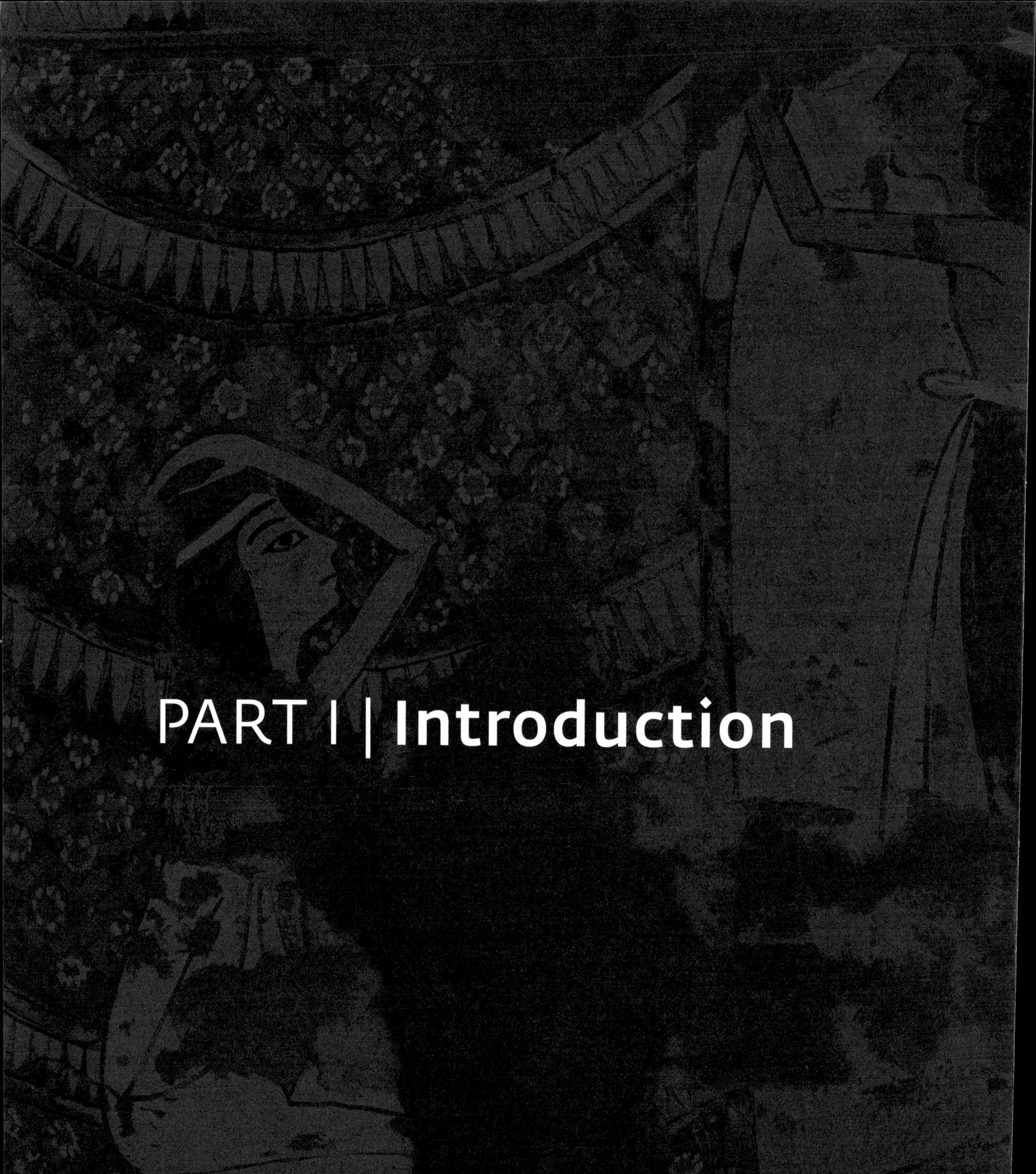

PART I | Introduction

1. Hair in the funerary contexts of Ancient Egypt

1.1 Iconography and Texts

We have all become familiar with scenes on the Ancient Egypt tomb walls depicting funerary ceremonies. The Egyptian artists often immortalized the procession where many mourners are lamenting the death of the deceased, next to the coffin. According to the iconography and religious texts these mourners, who are mainly women, showed a very characteristic body language; they did not only cry, they also hit their arms, beat their bodies, poured mud on their heads, ripped their clothes and pulled or shook their hair. This shaking of the hair attracted my attention. While carefully observing the decoration in many tombs and studying *papyri,* I found that the following scene was repeated many times: women covering their faces with a large lock of their hair. In this book I will present my research on this ritual and I will attempt to make a general reconstruction of the Ancient Egyptian funerary ritual.

Already from the Old Kingdom, both literary and representational references to mourning can be found. The *Pyramid Texts* for instance give references to mourners as well as to hair. However, the tomb decoration from this period does not offer many usable examples for clear analysis. The artists of the Old Kingdom also presented some moments of mourning, but they were not as explicit as in later periods. Nevertheless, some tomb owners did have their mourners immortalized in reliefs. This is for instance the case for Mereruka in Saqqara or Idu in Giza, both dated to Dynasty VI. In the mastaba tomb of Mereruka, there is a scene on the south wall of the main offering chamber where a group of women is mourning. Among them there is one woman who is pulling a frontal lock of hair (fig. 5). The mastaba of Idu in Giza has mourning scenes at the entrance of the main chamber. In those scenes both men and women appear to be mourning and some of them are pulling locks of hair as well (fig. 6).

↓ Fig. 5
Mourning women from the tomb of Mereruka. Saqqara. Dynasty VI. Photo: María Rosa Valdesogo

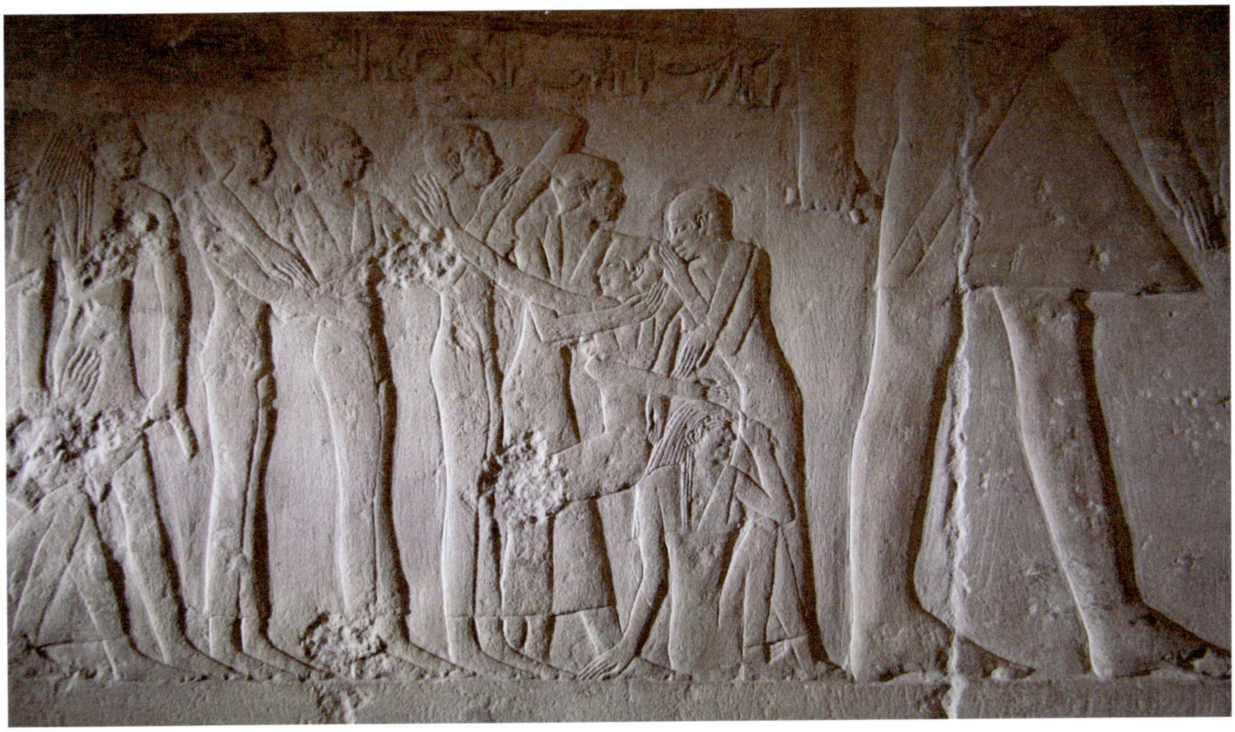

← Fig. 6
Mourning women from the tomb of Idu. Giza. Dynasty VI (After Simpson, *The Mastabas of Qar and Idu* G. 7101 and G. 7102. Boston, 1976).

Since we are looking at the funerary sphere, it is pivotal to also consider the principal funerary texts from Ancient Egypt, and having analysed them, I found many references to hair, especially in the *Coffin Texts* of the Middle Kingdom. And if religious texts from the Middle Kingdom provide us with good literary evidence, then what is happening with the iconography of that period? While looking for examples of depictions of mourners I found two important depictions from the Middle Kingdom: one of them (a fragment of a coffin from Abydos (ca 1550 BCE), The Fritzwilliam Museum in Cambridge, E.283.1900) shows the representation of a mourner with dishevelled hair beside a coffin, leaning towards it. Another depiction is found on the Louvre stela C15 (stele of Abkaou) from Dynasty XI where two women who assist the dead are gesturing in similar ways (fig. 4).

↓ Fig. 4
Stele of Abkaou from Abydos. Dynasty XI. Paris, Musée du Louvre, C15. Photo: ©RMN-Grand Palais.

From later periods, one of the most explicit documents is the vignette in Chapter 168 of the *Book of the Dead* in the Papyrus of Sethnakht (fig.1), dated to Dynasty XIX. A very similar image can be seen in the Papyrus of Muthetepti however, dating to the Third Intermediate Period. According to these texts there are mourning women in the procession of Re and they are shaking their hair and covering their faces with it. Many other documents demonstrate that these were not isolated cases.

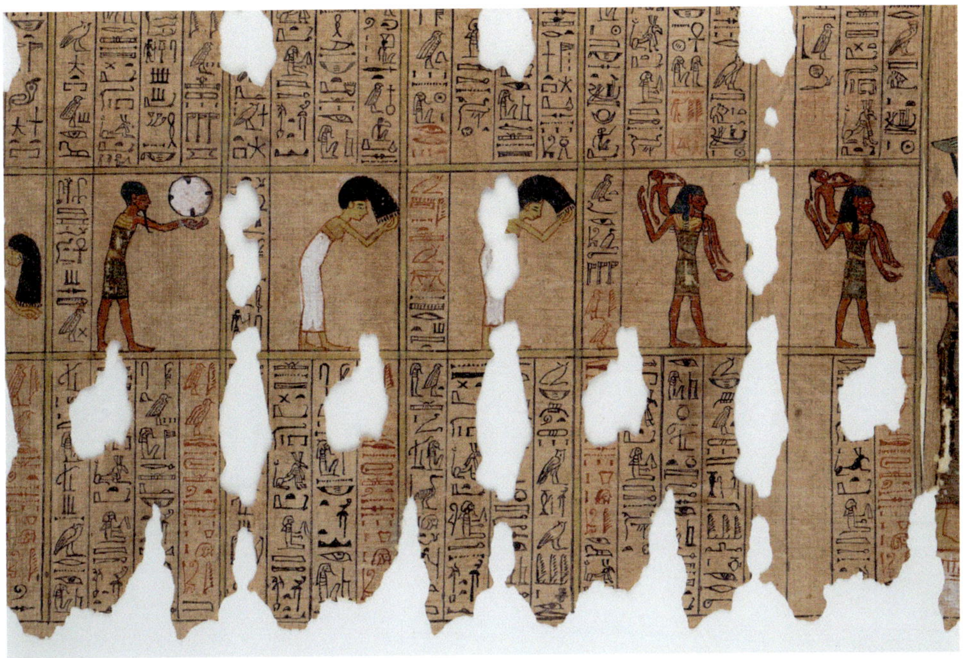

→ Fig. 1
Funerary Papyrus of the steward Sethnakht. Procedence unknown. Dynasty XIX. Metropolitan Museum of Art of New York, 35.9.19a-e. Photo: Metropolitan Museum of Art of New York.

In some Theban tombs from the New Kingdom we can find funerary scenes where mourning women are gesticulating in a similar manner: Amenemhat (TT82), Minakht (TT87), Rekhmire (TT100) (fig. 2) and Ineni (TT81), as well as in the tomb of Renni at el-Kab. And although not in a tomb - but nevertheless in the funerary context - there is a similar scene from the mortuary temple of Seti I in Dra Abu el-Naga (fig. 3). Such a widely depicted comportment cannot be a mere coincidence or a theatrical exposure of pain or a trend in decoration among artists; it has to arise from a deeper reason, related to funerary rites.

→ Fig. 2
Mourning women from the tomb of Rekhmire (TT100). Thebes. Dynasty XVIII. Photo: María Rosa Valdesogo.

↑ Fig. 3
Mourning women at both ends of the corpse; from the funerary temple of Seti I in Dra Abu el-Naga (Thebes). Dynasty XIX. Photo Mª Rosa Valdesogo

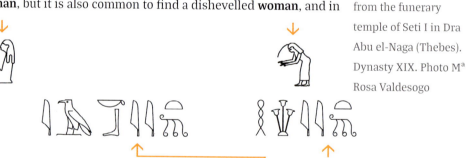

Apart from the iconography it is also necessary to look into the descriptions used accompanying these depictions. The most common words used in the Egyptian language for "mourner" were *iꜣkbyt* and *ḥꜣyt*. In many cases the writing included the determinative of a sitting **woman**, but it is also common to find a dishevelled **woman**, and in many cases the word is written with the hieroglyph for hair at the end: (*iꜣkbyt*), (*ḥꜣyt*). This shows that their hair was such an important part of these women, that it could even identify them.

Finally, in the *Coffin Texts*, a 'common denominator' can be found: in all chapters mentioning hair, female mourners are the main actors and - together with the mourning rite - the Osiris myth appears as the backdrop. All the iconography shows a direct connection of hair with the dead and the funerary ceremony. Taking this into consideration, the concepts we have to combine and consider in this research are: death, Osiris, resurrection, mourning woman and hair.
Another factor drew my attention to Egyptian mourning women. In many tombs from

the New Kingdom the two mourners in the role of Isis and Nephthys standing at both ends of the coffin appear during the funeral procession, with their heads (and thus their hair) covered with the *ꜥfnt* head-dress. These two women at the end of the funerary ceremony are represented with short hair kneeling in front of the four ponds and offering globular vases (fig. 7). I will go deeper into this aspect later, in the third part of this book and explain its meaning.

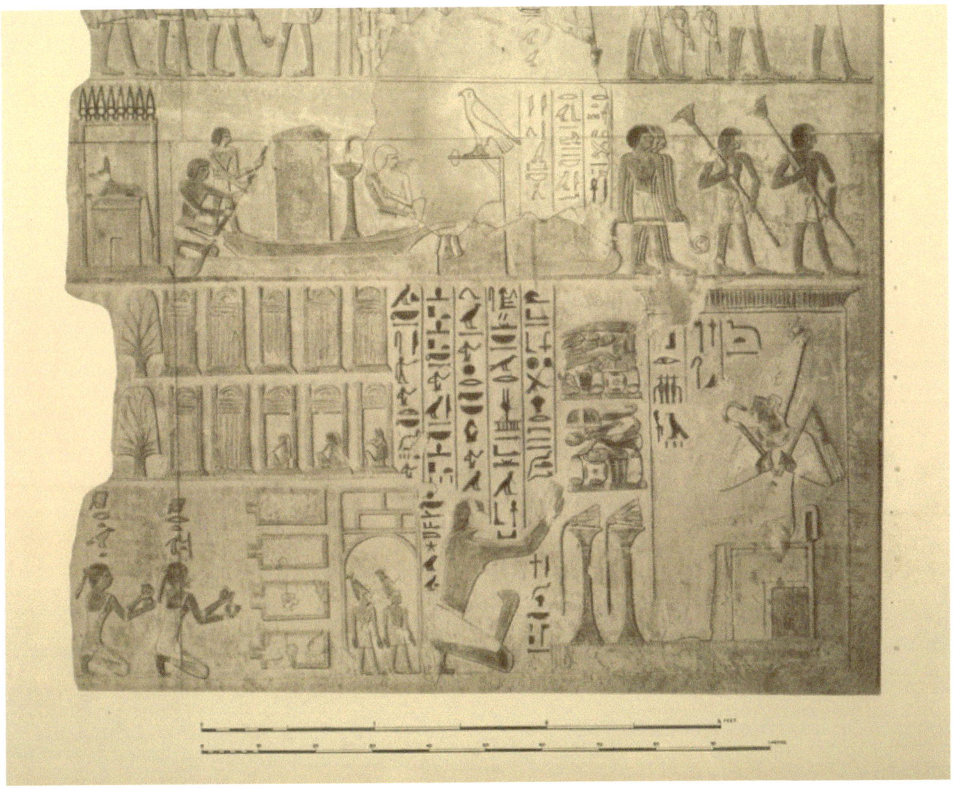

→ Fig. 7
The two mourning women (*ḏrty*) from the tomb of Pahery (EK3). El-Kab. Dynasty XVIII (After Taylor and Griffith, *The Tomb of Paheri at el-Kab.* EEF. London, 1894).

1.2 Archaeological finds of loose hair offerings from funerary contexts

Apart from texts, I have also looked at some archaeological remains of hair found in certain tombs to see if these remains could be related to mourning practices. In different periods of Egyptian history, hair offerings for the deceased can be found. Petrie found a plait of hair and a false fringe in the tomb of King Djer (Dynasty I) in Abydos, which, according to him, belonged to a queen.[1] There is also a commoner's grave in Abydos, probably dating to Dynasty III, containing many locks of hair, some of them plaited and some knotted.[2] In Balabish, south of Abydos, there is a necropolis dating to the New Kingdom and later. Near the Nile floodplain, some graves from the Middle Kingdom were found as well. In tomb group B213 an oval grave (pan-grave) contained some short plaits of hair close to the mummy, but they could also have belonged to the deceased.[3] In the tomb of Tutankhamun a plait of hair belonging to the Queen Tiye was found inside a small anthropoid sarcophagus. According to A. Rowe, it could be a relic of a deified queen, so

1 Petrie, 1902, p.5, pl. IV, fig.7. These remains are nowadays in the Pitt Rivers Museum of Oxford.

2 Maspero, 1912, p.170

3 Wainwright, 1920, p.11.

that the plait was considered the hair of a goddess.[4] Considering the fact that Queen Tiye was already dead when Tutankhamun was buried, it seems much more logical to think of it as a family relic[5] not having any relationship with a funerary rite. In Deir el-Bahari a group of tombs from Dynasties XVII, XVIII and XIX is located. Maspero confirms that locks of hair were wrapped and buried between the legs, arms and around the necks of each mummy.[6] In a tomb in Deir el-Medina several locks of hair were found inside a basket.[7] In the tomb of Queen Merit-Amon in Deir el-Bahari,[8] dating to Dynasty XVIII, H. E. Winlock found three baskets with human locks and plaits of hair inside. Since they were found together with some other toiletry objects, Winlock thought this hair to be for Merit-Amon's hairdressing in the Hereafter,[9] a logical assumption.

In many houses in Amarna, clay balls with hair inside were found. At el-Kahun in the year 1890, Petrie found two clay balls with locks of hair in a tomb dating to Dynasty XX.[10] For some scholars they could have been utilised for some kind of domestic magic.[11] However, there is a very well argued suggestion of G. Tassie. According to him the clay balls with the hair symbolised a contract between the deceased and the priesthood granting that the funerary rituals were done properly.[12]

In Deir el-Bahari a mummy of a young girl was found dating to Dynasty XXI. Locks of hair of 40 cm in length were placed between her legs.[13] In Gurob Tomb 605 a squared case, which contained locks of hair, was located at the feet of a female mummy. Hair remains were found in other tombs there as well.[14] Finally, the Douch necropolis in el-Kharga,[15] dating to the I-Vth century CE, should be mentioned. Ten tombs contained deposits with globular clay vases with cut hair wrapped in cloth packs inside.[16] These vases were sometimes found on the ground and sometimes inside a hole in the wall of the burial chamber. According to the investigating scholars, the hair inside did not belong to the mummies, since they still had their own hair, but were offerings from different persons. This list is not exhaustive, and throughout Egypt many other swats of loosc hair have been found in funerary context. The exact meaning of these locks of hair and the reason why they were deposited inside ancient tombs is not clear at this moment and need further research. However, it is tempting to consider them in future analysis in relation to the function of hair in the funerary and mourning rituals and in

4 Rowe, 1941, p.624.

5 Nachtergael, 1980, p.243.

6 Maspero, 1893, p.274.

7 Wagner *et allii*, 1984-1985, p.188. They are now in the Musée du Louvre (Département des Antiquités Égyptiennes, Inv. Nº E 18851).

8 TT 358.

9 Winlock, 1932, p.34, Pl. XXXII y XXXIII.

10 Crompton, 1916, p.128. They are in the Manchester Museum.

11 Peet and Woolley, 1923, p.66.

12 Tassie, 1996, p.61.

13 Daressy, 1907, p.34.

14 Bell, 1985, pp. 61-86, Pl. II.

15 Dunand, Heim, Henein, Lichtenberg, 1992; Wagner et *allii*, 1984-1985, pp.175-202.

16 The tombs are: T3, T4, T5, T7, T9, T11, T12, T53, T58, T66.

relation to hair offerings that are mentioned in ancient texts, which I address in detail in this publication.
Taking into consideration the archaeological data, the texts and the iconography, it becomes clear that the mourner's hair received special attention and treatment during the ancient Egyptian funerals and the funerary sphere. The objective of this research was to further understand this kind of attention, what the specific treatment was and why.

2. Hair and symbolism

As we have seen, the Egyptian words referring to mourners use the hieroglyph of a woman (a dishevelled woman) or even hair as a determinative, showing the importance of that element in the mourning rite. It is not unusual to find similar symbols in other cultures, separated in time and space. According to anthropologists, there is a connection between collective knowledge and the individual subconsciousness that allows some symbols to become universal.[17] For instance, water is an element that is always related to concepts of purification, fertility and renewal. The same holds true for hair: it can symbolise similar things in dissimilar societies and it usually receives special treatment in ceremonies and rituals.

Hair is very easy to handle and modify; in ceremonies from different cultures it is treated in such a way that it reflects a change of state or condition in a person's life. This is reflected for instance by hair that is cut when a person reaches puberty or when an adult joins a religious order. The loss of hair (due to sickness, alopecia, accidents, etc.) implies failure and has a negative connotation.[18] However, when this loss is consciously and deliberately made by human hand, it connotes a sacrifice. It is a voluntary mutilation, which simulates a renunciation of oneself by means of a kind of corporeal "amputation".[19] The sacrifice of hair consists of two acts: 1) to cut it, implying being differentiated from the rest and 2) to dedicate it, implying being united with the sacred world.[20]

Hair is also a natural protection for the head.[21] The head is universally considered to be the centre of vital energy and intellect (I use this as a more universal theory here; since in ancient Egypt the head was not considered to be the centre of intellect), since it issues speech, which pronounces thoughts and the creation of words.[22] In the same manner as nails can be cut and grow back, hair falls out and grows back spontaneously, as if it restores itself. Thanks to this property of auto-regeneration, hair is often considered to be a symbol of power as well. Hair has its own vitality and for that reason hair is considered a symbol of health and growth. Hair is thus a manifestation of energy and it is related to the force of life itself.[23]

17 Hershman, 1974, p.274.
18 Cirlot, 1991, p.111.
19 Chevalier and Gheerbrandt, 1969, p.366.
20 Van Gennep, 1909, p.238.
21 Naguib, 1990, p.9.
22 Naguib, 1990, p.23.
23 Cirlot, 1991, p.111.

On the other hand, hair also identifies its owner and is relevant from a social point of view[24]. Hair and nails can be cut without pain, and after this separation, hair is still closely related to the person from whom it originated.[25] Hair is also closely linked to fertility and sensuality. Maybe for that reason hair is often intimately related to women, and a woman's hair is often considered an attractive feature.[26] Since hair is linked to fecundity, it is also associated with vegetation. In fact, for agricultural communities hair growth is often connected to alimentary plant growth.[27]

Taking all this hair symbolism into consideration, I believe that Ancient Egyptian images of mourning women with dishevelled hair were not just an aspect of funerals, but may have had a deeper meaning. If these scenes were so common in the Egyptian funerary iconography, it was because tomb owners had chosen them, and the reason for their choice underlined the importance and deeper meaning. We know that Ancient Egyptian art was not gratuitous at all; every figure, every scene, every statue, etc. had a reason and a function. Thus, the dishevelled Egyptian mourners must have had a deeper meaning related to the funerary sphere in which they were depicted.

Some Egyptian words found in the textual sources referring to hair are repeated constantly: the hair *smꜣ*, the lock of hair *swt*, the long hair (mane) *sꜣmt*, the two

curls *wprt*, the braid *ḥnskt*. And religious texts from different periods of Egyptian history also share similar passages. Repetition in texts but also in iconography lets us to believe that we are on the verge of discovering a custom with two dimensions: both ritual and symbolic. It is now necessary to combine all the existing evidence in order to obtain a complete picture of this ritual and symbolic meaning and discover what the Egyptian artists and scribes were hinting at with these images and phrases.

3. Mourning women in Ancient Egyptian funerals

Scholars have extensively written about Ancient Egyptian mourners as women who cried and lamented the death of a loved-one at funerals. These female mourners accompanied the coffin during the procession to the necropolis and they were characterized by

24 Tassie, G.J.; (2009). The social and ritual contextualisation of Ancient Egyptian hair and hairstyles from the Protodynastic to the end of the Old Kingdom. Doctoral thesis. UCL (University College London).

25 Chevalier and Gheerbrandt, 1969, p.366. For instance in Japan, during XVI and XVII centuries, when someone died, relatives cut a lock of hair and the nails of the deceased.

26 Chevalier and Gheerbrandt, 1969, p.369.

27 Chevalier and Gheerbrandt, 1969, p.369.

their behaviour: raising the arms, beating themselves, ripping their clothes and making gestures which expressed their sadness and desperation. Reading the funerary texts, we can further assume that they always refer to the same group of women, since they commonly mention the *i͗ꜣkbyt* or *ḥꜣyt*; and among these mourners was, without a doubt,

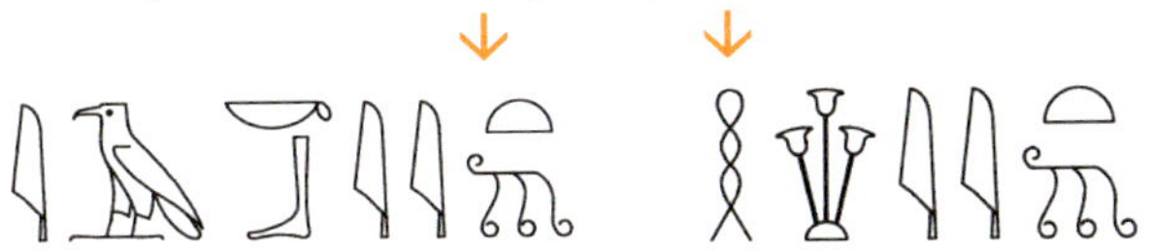

also the widow, lamenting the loss of her husband. But this often remains a very generic description of who these women were and what they did during the ceremony. If we pay attention to Egyptian tomb scenes of funerary processions (the best examples come from tombs and from some *papyri* from the New Kingdom) we realize that not all women in these scenes had the same function, nor were they always together or depicted doing similar things. In the scenes of funerary processions, we can usually observe different types of mourning women:

Firstly, a group of mourning women (also men in the New Kingdom) are presented behind the coffin on the way to the tomb. These are the mourners wailing, hitting their bodies and ripping their clothes. They are presented all together in an inhomogeneous and disordered group. We can imagine them making noise, maybe in a chaotic performance. These are the kind of mourners we find from the Old Kingdom onwards, for example in the mastabas of Mereruka or Idu (figs. 5 and 6), to the later periods of Egyptian history.

Secondly, the close relatives - we can assume - would be most grieved about the beloved's death. Due to the fact that most of the preserved tombs belonged to men, their death would presumably be particularly sad for the widows. On the tomb scenes, next to

→ Fig. 8
The widow and the two professional mourners from the tomb of Roy (TT255). Thebes. Dynasty XIX. Photo: María Rosa Valdesogo.

the coffin of the funeral processions, kneeling or standing women are depicted, who are described as the wife, widow or servant (fig. 8) of the tomb owner. They stand apart from the large group of mourers, but they wail in a similar fashion.

Finally, there are two mourning women always standing at both ends of the coffin, who are described as *ḏrty* (*"The two kites"*) or as Isis and Nephthys (fig. 8). These women personify the two goddesses and appear to be assisting the corpse during the procession to the tomb. Although they also mourn the deceased (these representatives of Isis and Nephthys make very typical mourning gestures), their behaviour is apparently more moderate.

As shown, we find three different types of mourning women in the Ancient Egyptian funerary ceremony, and according to the documents also mentioned in the introduction, all of them shook or pulled their hair during the funeral. With this research I would like to establish why these women made these gestures with their hair.

Another interesting feature is how these women were represented during the different periods of Egyptian history. Taking a look at scenes from the Old Kingdom to the later periods makes us realize that there are distinct differences. In the mastabas of the elite in the Old Kingdom, funerary processions were represented in a less explicit way than later on. In these mastabas we can see groups of women (in Idu's tomb also men) lamenting and crying and making common mourning gestures. As stated before, the *ḏrty* mourners could also be a part of the funeral, but they appear at both ends of the coffin, set apart from the rest of the mourners.

There are not many examples of funerary procession from Middle Kingdom tombs, however some isolated documents (for instance the fragment of a coffin from Abydos now in

← Fig. 9
The two *ḏrty* with the corpse from the tomb of Antefoker (TT60). Thebes. Dynasty XII (After Garis Davies, *The Tomb of Antefoker, vizier of Sesostris I, and his Wife Senet (No. 60)*. EES. London, 1920)

The Fritzwilliam Museum in Cambridge, E.283.1900) show that the custom of shaking the hair was still practiced in that period of Egyptian history. During funerals, the two mourners called *ḏrty* also accompanied the corpse and were set apart from the rest of the group of mourners (fig. 9).

During the New Kingdom, artistic expression is more prolific and the decorative program on the tomb walls is richer than in the previous periods. The funerary ceremony from Dynasty XVIII appears more detailed than before. The scenes of the procession now show many members taking part in the funeral and the artists even include scenes of the Opening of the Mouth Ceremony. The group of mourners seems to be bigger and includes young girls as well, all of them crying, raising their arms and in some cases shaking their hair. In the late New Kingdom, the men are also shown mourning the deceased, but they do not appear shaking or pulling their hair. Those tombs from the New Kingdom also show the two mourners *ḏrty* accompanying the coffin apart from the group of - what I shall from now on call - 'common mourners' and also having an active part during the Opening of the Mouth Ceremony. Many of these scenes are described in more detail below.

So, as centuries went by, the iconography became more explicit and provides us with much more details of what happened during the funerary ceremony. This helps us to discern the roles of the different mourners who lamented and shook or pulled their hair. Finally, Egyptian iconography shows two main gestures made by mourning women with their hair: shaking a mane of hair forwards and pulling a frontal lock of hair. But how do religious texts mention these practices? Comparing the different funerary texts from Ancient Egypt, I found that the *Coffin Texts* from the Middle Kingdom provided most references to this subject. For that reason, they were the starting point of my research.

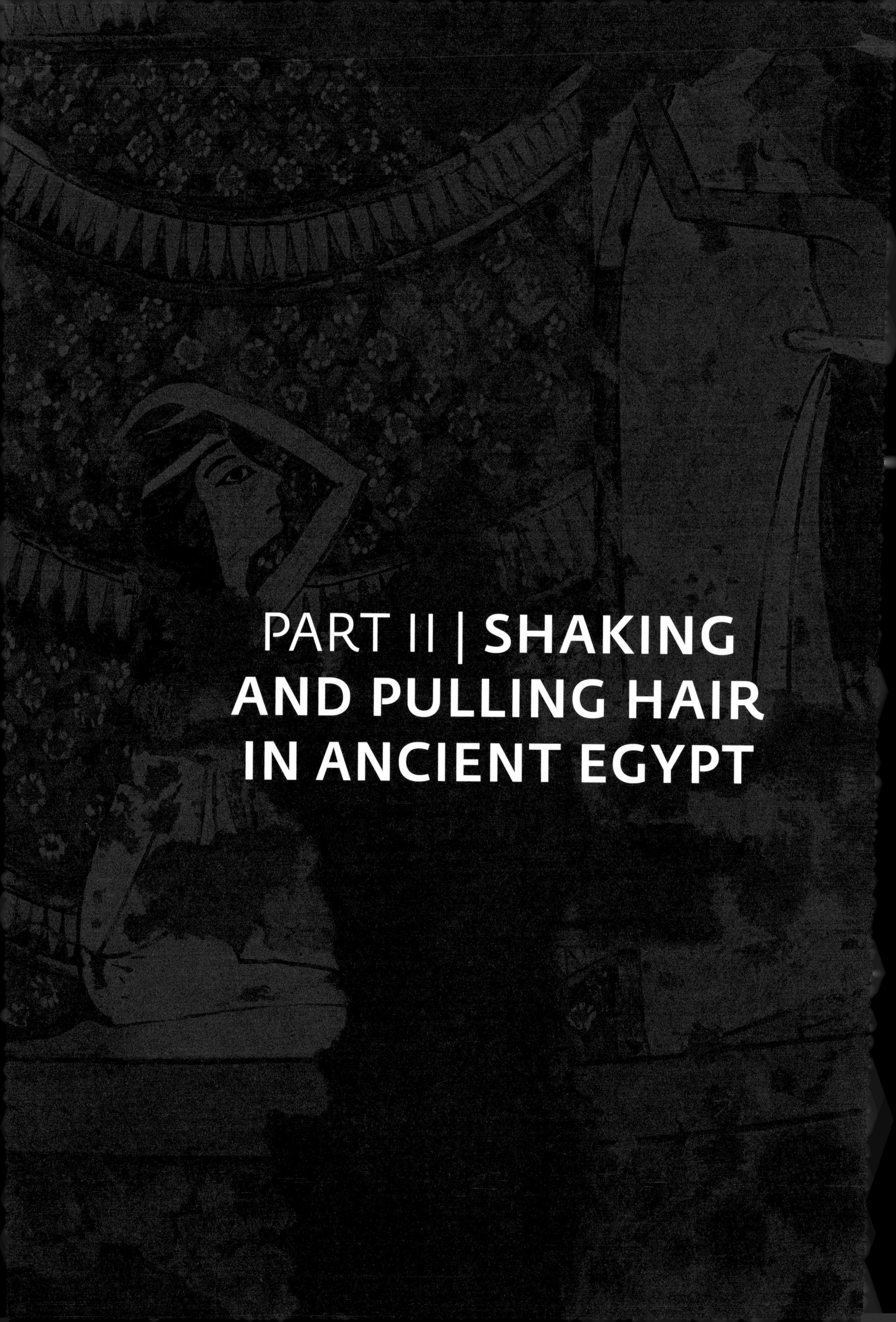

PART II | SHAKING AND PULLING HAIR IN ANCIENT EGYPT

1. Mourning women shake their hair

We will now look at the different texts that mention female mourners shaking or pulling their hair. Four spells of the *Coffin Texts* of the Middle Kingdom mention how the female mourners shake their hair, *smꜣ*, for the deceased and apparently "for his benefit". In Chapter 66 the gesture of shaking the hair is made by the two goddesses Isis and Nephthys: *"...Isis is nursing you; Nephthys gives her breast facing down...The Two Ladies of Dep*[28] *give you their hairs... (di n.k Nbty Dp smꜣw.sn*[29]*)."* It is interesting to note how the word for "The Two Ladies" (*Nbty*) can be also written with the determinative of a dishevelled person.[30] This hieroglyph is a determinative in the verbs *nwn*[31] (also *wnwn*)

or *sps*[32], which mean "to mess one's hair up or cover the face with the hair as sign of mourning", a gesture made by mourning women.[33]

As stated before, artists from the Old Kingdom depicted scenes of funeral processions with women making special gestures as a sign of mourning, like raising their arms, beating their heads, putting their hands on their chests and pulling the hair (figs. 6 and 7). In the *Pyramid Texts* of the Old Kingdom those scenes are described as: *"The souls of Buto rock for you; they beat their bodies and their arms for you, they pull their hair for you (nwn.sn n.k m smꜣw.sn*[34]*)"*.[35] Although the expression here includes the preposition *m* after the verb[36], it still shows a special gesture with the hair, *smꜣ*, during the lament; and the choice of the verb *nwn* is similar to what is mentioned in the *Coffin Texts*.
Moving forward in time, we find similar expressions in the *Book of the Dead* of the New Kingdom: *"...mourners have dishevelled for you*[37] *(i(ꜣ)kbywt wnwn.sn ḥr.k),*[38] *they beat with their arms for you, they scream for you, they cry for you..."*.[39] Both words and determinatives recall the funerary scenes in Chapter 168 of the *Book of the Dead* of Muthetepti. Here, the passage describes a procession in which the gods of the Hereafter are following Re-Osiris and among them are the "*Mourners of Re*". These mourners are depicted shaking their hair forwards (*nwn smꜣ*). This was a typical gesture made by mourning women.

28 Pe and Dep were the city of Buto in Lower Egypt.

29 

30 

31 *Wb* II, 222, 5.

32 *Wb* IV, 107, 9.

33 Men usually let their beard and hair grow up for some days (Desroches-Noblecourt, 1947, p.230) and still the Egyptian *fellahs* did that during the last century (Blackman, 1948, p.58).

34 

35 *Pyr.*1005, 1974.

36 Nwn m can also be translated as "*pull from*" (Faulkner, 1962, p. 128, 2). It is used in New Kingdom documents, although not with the hair smA, but with lock of hair swt.

37 Or "*over you*".

38 

39 *BD*, 180.

In order to better understand the real meaning of some of these practices it is necessary to observe what is shown next to the gesture of shaking hair forwards, in front of the face. In Chapter 66 of the *Coffin Texts* two actions appear to happen simultaneously: the "giving" of the hair and the nursing of the dead. During the funerary procession in Ancient Egypt it was very common to pour some milk on the road by which the coffin was passing (fig. 10). This had a strong symbolic meaning, because milk is the first nourishment of a child given by his mother. In a way this deed resembled an act of resurrection. Isis brings the deceased back to life, and death becomes a new birth. And this happens while Isis and Nephthys present their hair *smꜣ*. In fact, thinking of the prone body of the dead, we could also consider the expression "*give the hair*" a metaphor of "*bending over him*", and the gesture of shaking the hair could be somehow related to the concept of maternity.

→ Fig. 10
Pouring liquid (milk or water) in the transport of the deceased's statue. Tomb of Maja. Saqqara. Dynasty XVIII. Berlin, Neues Museum, ÄM 2089/2. Photo María Rosa Valdesogo.

In Chapter 991 of the *Coffin Texts*, the dead is assimilated with the crocodile god Sobek, who says about himself: *"I am a master of glory...to whom the mourners give their hair (ddw n.f smwt.f smꜣw.sn)*[40]*...I am the one who ejaculates over the mourners (ink sṯw ḥr smwt).*"[41] Until now we have read terms like *ỉꜣkbwt*[42] or *ḥꜣyt*;[43] which derive from verbs that mean "*to regret*". But in this chapter the word for "*mourners*" is *smwt.*[44] This term seems phonetically closer to *smꜣ* or *sꜣmt*, words that mean "*sorrow*" or "*lament*",[45] but also "*lock of hair*".[46] This would approximate the figure of the mourner to hair as a representative element from a phonetic point of view. Since the text states that the deceased impregnates the mourners, there is a new aspect that appears to be included in the context of mourning and dishevelled women: sex. In the Egyptian funerary context, sex played a very important role. According to the Myth of Osiris, Isis contributed to the god's resurrection by placing herself over his phallus thus conceiving Horus. It is an act of giving life, although now the dead is the one who has this life-giving ability. We will see throughout this research that this sexual element is inseparable from the mourners and their lamentation.

In Chapter 167 of the *Coffin Texts* the dead is called *Mḫnty-n-ỉrty*[47] and he receives food offerings in order to feed his *ka*. In this chapter the dead addresses the mourner directly, saying: "*...mourner! Get your hair ready for me (ḥꜣyt ỉr n.ỉ smꜣ.ṯ).*[48]" Here the mourners do not give (*rdỉ*) their hair, as we have read before, but they have it ready (*ỉrỉ*) for the deceased. The expression *ỉrỉ smꜣ* could refer to "*brush*", "*clear out*", "*arrange*", but it does not seem to refer to the gesture of shaking hair forwards as we have seen before. It is very important to note that in this chapter the offerings to the dead were given during two festivals: *snwt* and *dnỉt*. These were lunar feasts in which the Ancient Egyptians celebrated the recovery of the Eye of Horus after the battle against Seth. In this we find another important element related to hair and which appears frequently: the moon.

The text of Chapter 674 of the *Coffin Texts* is less clear, but it also treats the lunar festivities *snwt* and *dnỉt* and the food offerings for the mummy. In this context we read that the mouth of the deceased is "*...like the knife ds*[49] *in Beni Hassan in front of the living ones.*

40 

41 

42 

43 

44 

45 Meeks, 1977-1979, II, p.306, 78.3294; *Wb* IV, 18, 10.

46 Faulkner, 1962, p.210.

47 It means "*The one who is in front of the two eyes*" and it was initially a falcon-shaped god, but later it became a designation of Horus.

48 

49 The knife ds was used in sacrifices and here it is assimilated to the first quarter of the moon.

ẖspr(?), Ḳbt (?)[50], and his *"water is the hair of Mẖt over you (mw.ỉ smꜣ Mḫt ḥr.ṯn).*[51]*"* The *ds* knife was assimilated to the first quarter of the moon, so it was considered a defence against enemies. But the most important point is that we find the hair, *smꜣ*, likened to water, another vital element par excellence. In addition, it is relevant to note that the word *mw*, which primarily means "*water*", can also be translated in Egyptian as "*breast milk*"[52], so we would remain in the same revitalizing contextual meaning.
According to what we have read thus far, we can now deduce that the hair of the mourners played an important role in the funerary context of Ancient Egypt. Maybe with the gesture of shaking the hair, mourners activated the interrelation of many elements: water, hair (*smꜣ*), the moon, maternity and femininity; all of them were beneficial to the process of resurrection. At this point, it is obvious that hair had strong symbolism, which needs to be discussed further.

2. The symbolism of hair in ancient Egyptian belief

2.1.Hair as a symbol of water

2.1.1. Hair is the primordial water

There is a close relationship in the symbolic context between water and hair. "*From the moment that it is wavy, the hair recalls the aquatic image and vice versa*".[53] Regarding this matter it is important to point out that it was very common in Ancient Egypt to associate hair with the colour blue,[54] which was the preferred colour for water in artistic representation. And this is also acceptable the other way around, because the hieroglyph of water was usually black (fig. 11), the colour for the hair in Egyptian art.[55]

→ Fig. 11
Hieroglyph of water in black color. Detail from a coffin from Middle Kingdom. Beni Suef Museum. Photo: María Rosa Valdesogo.

50 Coldness?

51  We should expect here the preposition *m* (*mw.ỉ m smꜣ*...). But this is a nominal sentence with nouns (Allen, J.P., 2000, p.71.); it was not common in Middle Egyptian, but it was in the ancient language (Lefebvre, 1988, p.296). On the other hand, the way the preposition Hr is written is also unusual, since it was before a suffix pronoun

52 *Wb* II, 52, 8.

53 Durand, 1979, p.93.

54 In fact, in the Egyptian belief the hair of divinities was made of lapis lazuli (Aufrère, 1993, p.8).

55 Ransom Williams, 1932, p.59.

Hair that is related to water is exclusively women's hair, because the liquid element is feminine,[56] and water and menstruation are regulated by the lunar cycle. According to G. Durand, in a more general anthropological point of view, the moon is also linked to death and femininity, and this femininity is the reason why the moon is connected to water symbolism as well.[57] In this same line of thought F.A. Hassan affirms that in many cultures, women are linked to water; this is connected to the growth of grain, so metaphorically also to menstrual blood. He also asserts that this union between women and water appears in Egyptian Predynastic iconography, where feminine images are shown next to water signs, like shells.[58] In 1964, D. Bonneau associated the hair of Isis with the rise of the Nile due to the bushes of papyrus floating on it.[59] According to this scholar, in the Ancient Egyptian tradition the manes of the gods were bushes of papyrus and the locks of hair were the vegetable fibres that contain the first rise and announce the inundation of the river.[60] For that reason, D. Bonneau concludes that usually hair was linked to gods related to the Nile flood.[61]

This relationship between hair and water is already evident in the Old Kingdom when the *Pyramid Texts* of pharaoh Pepi I affirm that "*...the hair of Pepi is the Nun...*".[62] In fact, hair is inseparable from the aquatic element, since in water bodies without papyrus plants or reeds, Egyptians called the coralline formations along the shores of Red Sea and the Indian Ocean "*the hair of Isis*".[63] In Ancient Egyptian cosmogony water was the original element where the creation came from. And in the funerary processions, liquid was poured over the road by which the coffin was passing (fig. 10). According to the inscriptions next to those scenes, this liquid could be either milk or water. This action had two reasons, one practical and another symbolic. On the one hand the liquid prevented the sledge to get too hot because of friction with the ground and to facilitate the sliding; on the other hand it could symbolize the moment of creation, when order came from chaos.[64] The image of the coffin on top of the liquid recalls the first moment of the primordial hill coming out from the water. Furthermore, in the *Pyramid Texts* the Eye of Horus, which is offered to the dead Osiris, is considered to be similar to poured water, and this is also the milk of Isis.[65]

---

56 Menstruation is liquid.

57 Durand, 1979, p.95.

58 Hassan, 1992, p.314.

59 Bonneau, 1964, p.259.

60 Bonneau, 1964, p.260.

61 Bonneau, 1964, p. 260, n.9.

62 Budge, 1969, p.109.

63 *"Juba relates that near the Trogloditas Islands a brush grew deep down in the sea called "hair of Isis", without leaves and similar to coral"* (Pliny the Elder, *Natural History*, XIII, 51)

64 Enel, 1985, p.250.

65 *Pyr.* 371.

In this case we should pay attention to the verb nwn, utilized here for the gesture of shaking the hair forwards, and notice its sign placed between the two hieroglyphs of water. It is inevitable to assume a relationship between the *nwn* gesture of

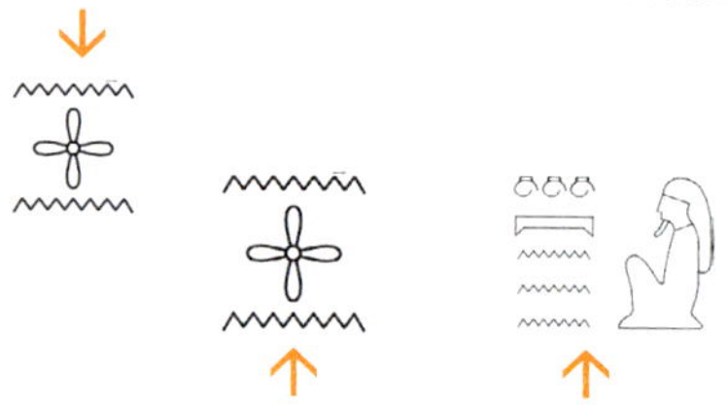

shaking the hair and the *Nwn*, the primordial chaos of Egyptian cosmogony (a word play also comes to mind). The dishevelled hair could easily be a way of returning to this primeval moment, to the chaotic waters *(Nwn),* where the primordial hill came out and where the demiurge created the world.

Water is also considered in many cultures as a resource to purify and restore, because it can eliminate, or wash away the past and return to an earlier state. In this context we cannot avoid thinking of the Nile inundation, which signified the beginning of the Egyptian year and the agricultural cycle, the subsistence of the Egyptian people. The water of the inundation had a magic power in itself: according to the Magical Papyrus Paris I, line 29, the sacrifice of male fowl was effective if it was done in *"a place where the Nile has already retired its water before anybody has stepped on it, or a place dipped completely by the water of the Nile, or a place flooded by the Nile in an accidental way"*.[66] So, it had to be a place soaked by those regenerating principles, in order to improve the magic. If the water had this magical power and was associated with hair, it makes sense to assume a magical attribute of hair as well.

A relationship seems evident between the rejuvenating rituals and the inundation, which was announced by Sothis, the brightest star that appeared in the morning sky just before sunrise between the seventeenth and the nineteenth of July.[67] The goddess Sothis was for Egyptians "*the one who rejuvenates the vegetation*"[68] and she was associated with Isis: *"Your sister Isis comes to you, happy with your love, you put her over your phallus, your semen goes up to her, sharp as Sothis, (like) Horus equipped coming out from you, like Horus who is in Sothis."*[69] On earth Isis announces the rise of the Nile with her hair, meanwhile Sothis does the same when she appears in the firmament. Isis is *"the one who makes the Nile to increase and flow, the one who makes the Nile to get bigger in this season".* [70] So, the mane of Isis would be a promise of resurrection, because it would be the image of the water that creates and rejuvenates. In the funerary rite it would emanate from the *nwn* gesture (next to the corpse) to the dead. That would suppose a return to the *Nun*, the primordial waters from which life emerged; in the same manner in which the Nile permits the constant regeneration of Egyptian life. To shake the hair forwards would thus be the announcement of a new creation, in the same manner in which the presence of Sothis would announce the beginning of the flood and the New Year.

---

66 Bonneau, 1964, p.285.

67 Bonneau, 1964, p.263.

68 *Pyr.* 477.

69 *Pyr.* 632. The sexual aspect will be considered later.

70 Budge, 1973, p.278.

Many years ago, S. Mayassis studied the meaning of hair in Egyptian belief.[71] According to him, the hair was a synonym of power[72] and Isis covered her face with her mane to profit from its force and allow others to do the same thing.[73] S. Mayassis also thought that the action of untying the hair was a way of putting the magical power of the knot aside,[74] so the force of the hair was released and joined the person.[75] Certainly, hair constitutes an element of power and vigour, but S. Mayassis did not take into consideration the fact that the power of Isis' mane comes from its association with the rejuvenating water of the flood. That would explain that the *nwn* gesture expressed by mourners in funerals was a revitalising gesture. It brought back the dead to the *Nun*, bringing him back to life, since the dead was *"the one who has been created in the Nun"*.[76]

In the month of *Khoiak*, the fourth month of the season *Akhet* (Inundation), the Mysteries of Osiris took place, a group of rites commemorating the Osiris Myth.[77] In all these rites, mourning had a relevant place: women representing Isis and Nephthys lamented at the moment a figurine of Osiris was made with earth and grain,[78] the seed in the figurine would then grow as a symbol of life and resurrection. During this festival of Osiris, the twenty-fifth day of the *Khoiak* month, the two representatives of Isis and Nephthys recited aloud a sacred song of mourning[79] just before the resurrection of Osiris.[80] Their lamentation was the prelude to the new life for Osiris, also evident in the rise of the Nile.[81] At an everyday funeral the performance made by mourning women would also be the step prior to the dead's resurrection.

Further, Pausanias stated that the tears of Isis could be considered the inundation of the Nile: *"Egyptians say that Isis weeps for Osiris when the river starts increasing; and when it floods the fields, they say that it is Isis's tears"*. [82] Once the Nile started to rise, Egyptians celebrated the Festival of Isis. She, mourning Osiris, caused with her tears the increase of the water level of the Nile.[83] In *The Songs of Isis and Nephthys*, when they mourn, we read: "*I am Isis I flood the land in that day*" .[84] Tears (in Ancient Egyptian *rmit)* had a strong creative power in Egyptian mythology, because mankind (*rmṯ*) is said to have derived from tears.[85] According to a myth dating to Dynasty XII, the god Re sent one of his two

71 Mayassis, 1955.

72 Mayassis, 1955, p.354.

73 Mayassis, 1955, p.354 and 362.

74 Mayassis, 1955, p.356.

75 Mayassis, 1955, p.362.

76 *CT*, 544.

77 This also shows the relationship between Osiris and the water.

78 Guglielmi, 1980, p.80.

79 They are included in *The Lamentations of Isis and Nephthys* (Pap. Berlin 3008) and *The Songs of Isis and Nephthys* (Pap. British Museum 10188).

80 Gaballa and Kitchen, 1969, p.45.

81 Kees, 1956, p.354.

82 Pausanias, *De Phocicis,* X, 32,10.

83 Frazer, 1914, Third Ed., p 33.

84 *Songs*...3,16.

85 Guglielmi, 1980, p.82.

eyes to fight against his enemy Apophis. That eye was taking a long time to come back, so it was replaced by another one. When the eye of Re came back from battle and saw another one in its place, it became very upset. This eye started crying and people came forth from its tears. For consoling its sorrow Re turned it into the *uraeus* and put it on his forehead.

According to B. Mathieu "*to come out from the eye*" (*pr m ỉrt*) is an Egyptian expression referring to weeping and he emphasizes the fact that mankind appears from sorrow.[86] The eye and the humidity coming out of it (tears) have the power of giving life: *"He has opened his eyes in the moment he was going out from the Nun. All these things arouse to existence from his eyes."*[87] That would explain the important role of the mourners during the funerary ritual; they shed their tears with a regenerating power that would help in the resurrection of the dead. We should also note the importance of the eye as a beneficial organ for the regeneration of the deceased.

So, if we assimilate the water, *Nwn*, with the hair, *smꜣ*, why not consider a relationship between the hair, *smꜣ*, and the *nwn* gesture as a beginning of new life? We may assume that the *nwn* gesture of shaking the hair could refer on one hand to the sorrow because of the dead, and on the other hand to rebirth and a new creation. Mourners could shake their hair forwards as a sign of despair but also as an image of the primeval and chaotic water, which have the power of giving life and creation. At this point, we have to consider some other Egyptian rites with an aim to rejuvenate, with similar practices: the Sed Festival and the Festival of the Valley, in order to establish a similar relationship between hair and rebirth.

2.1.2. *Hair and the nwn gesture in the Sed festival*

In the tomb of Kheruef in Thebes (TT192) dating to the reign of Amenhotep III there is a relief of the Sed festival celebrated by that pharaoh. According to the inscription, which describes the scene, a group of women is "*stretching out, facing the king and making the ceremony [Sed Festival] before the throne*" (*sṯꜣ ḥmwt m-bꜣḥ nsw r ỉrt ỉrw* [ ] *ḫft-ḥr n ṯnṯꜣt*).[88] Those women are performing a dance in front of Amenhotep III bending their bodies and, in some cases, covering their faces with their manes of hair (fig. 12).[89] The inscription just above the dancers could be a song, of which the meaning is related to their movements.[90]

The Sed Festival was a ceremony for renewing the pharaoh's power. The Sed Festival had six main parts: 1) the pharaoh is, during a procession, dressed with the Sed shroud, 2)

86 Mathieu, 1986, p.500.

87 Fragment on the South facade of the temple of Hathor in Dendera (el-Kordy, 1982, p.203).

88 

89 Fakhry, 1943, Pl. XL, p.497. On some *talatats* from Karnak, the Sed Festival of Akhenaton with dancing women making the same movements was depicted.

90 Fakhry, 1943, p.497. In the temple of Bubastis there are some fragments that relate to the Sed Festival; one of them shows a group of dancers with a small part of this song. (Naville, 1892, Pl. XIV).

← **Fig. 12**
Detail of the Sed Festival from the tomb of Kheruef (TT192). Thebes. Dynasty XVIII (After *The Tomb of Kheruef Theban Tomb 192*. The Oriental Institute. University of Chicago. 1980)

rites of renewal and rebirth, 3) homage is paid to the rejuvenated pharaoh on his throne, 4) the pharaoh starts the new order of the world, 5) the pharaoh visits the gods in their chapels and 6) a ritual run of the pharaoh demonstrating his physical vigour.[91] Summed up, there was an initial ritual death of the king after which he came back to life with all his faculties and in perfect physical conditions to continue his kingship. The Sed Festival is a death-and-resurrection ceremony, in which some dancing women make the *nwn* gesture with their hair, and it could have a very deep symbolic meaning. The pharaoh is dead (although just metaphorically) and he has to be revived. In this case the Sed Festival is a ceremony of death and resurrection, so those dancers could be very closely related to the mourners in the funerary ceremony.

The Sed Festival has a Predynastic origin[92] and seems to be closely related to the cult of Osiris. On the Palermo Stone the register related to king Den shows the name of the god *Sed* written with the determinative of the *Upuaut* standard, the divinity that represents the king as first-born son,[93] so the god Sed could be an archaic version of *Upuaut "The opener of the ways"*. This idea is reinforced by the fact that in the festival of Osiris in Abydos, the one avenging the death of his father was not Horus, but *Upuaut.*[94] It is also possible that the Sed Festival in the Old Kingdom contained some elements of the cult of Osiris.[95] In the *Dramatic Ramesseum Papyrus*, recounting the ascension of Sesostris I to the throne of Egypt, we read that the erection of the *djed* pillar (an Osirian rite) was a very important moment in the Sed Festival.[96] Furthermore, there are many examples of iconography from the New Kingdom showing the relationship between the cult of Osiris and the Sed Festival as well.[97]

---

91 *LÄ* V, col. 785.

92 *LÄ* V, col. 782. The Sed Festival is documented from the beginning of the I Dynasty on the Narmer macehead and possibly also on the Scorpion macehead (Cervelló Autuori, 1996, p.209, n.154).

93 Cervelló Autuori, 1996, p.208, n.150.

94 Cervelló Autuori, 1996, p.210.

95 *LÄ* V, col. 786.

96 *LÄ* V, col. 786; Barta, 1976, pp.31-43.

97 *LÄ* V, col. 786.

There was also a relationship between the Sed Festival and the beginning of the inundation.[98] In the tomb of Kheruef (New Kingdom) we read: *"...Appearance of (King Amenhotep)...for resting on his throne that was in his Sed palace, built by him on the west side of the city. Opening the way through H.M. over the water of the flood, for bringing the gods of the Sed Festival."*[99] The Sed Festival was celebrated before the appearance of Sothis in the sky announcing that the annual flood of the Nile was coming. The inundation was one of the best examples of annual renewal for the Egyptians, because the floodwater contains mud that fertilizes the earth and grants the maintenance of the Egyptian people.

In conclusion, the inundation, as the water of *Nun* in the Egyptian cosmogony, contains the active ingredients for new life. The *Sed* festival was celebrated neither during the rise nor during the decrease of the flow, but at the driest moment,[100] just before the rising of Sothis and the arrival of the inundation. The Sed Festival announced the future waters, so it was the prelude of the new era, a new revival after the drought. And in the rite this announcement was linked to the group of dancers making the *nwn* gesture of shaking their hair forwards. During the Sed Festival, the pharaoh was like a ritually deceased who had to come back to life,[101] in this way he was assimilated to Osiris. That would explain the Osirian character of the ceremony. The king, symbolically dead, received the rites for revival that Isis, Nephthys, Anubis, Thot and Horus made over the corpse.[102] In this regenerating ritual the *nwn* gesture appeared as part of the practices for the rebirth of Osiris or pharaoh.

2.1.3. The hair and the nwn gesture in the Festival of the Valley

The Festival of the Valley was documented for the first time in the temple of Mentuhotep II (Middle Kingdom) in Deir el-Bahari as a Theban funerary feast in honour of the deceased. People visited the necropolis, decorated the tombs and carried offerings to their dead relatives. In the divine sphere the image of the god Amon was carried out of the temple of Karnak in his sacred barque (*wsr-ḥꜣt*)[103] and crossed the Nile to visit every mortuary temple of the West Bank. In the procession accompanying Amon were female priests, among whom there were several dancing women. According to a relief from the Red Chapel of Hatshepsut (New Kingdom) in Karnak[104] these women shook their hair forwards during the procession, making a *nwn* gesture like during the Sed Festival (fig. 13).

The Festival of the Valley took place during the summer solstice, between the harvest

98 Hornung und Staehelin, 1974, p.56.

99 Translation of Helck, 1966, p.78. Many documents show the relationship of Sothis with the Sed Festival: on a statue of the New Kingdom we read who the owner is *"beloved of Sothis, Lady of the Sed Festival"* and on the ceiling of the Ramesseum Ramses II sees Sothis *"at the beginning of the year, the Sed Festival and the flood"* (*AH* 1, 1974, p.58).

100 *AH* 1, p.58.

101 Mayassis, 1957, p.226.

102 Mayassis, 1957, p.68.

103 With the ones of Mut and Khonsu.

104 Michalowski, 1970, phot. 70.

and the inundation season. It coincided with the rising of Sothis in the sky announcing the arrival of the flood.[105] People, who visited the tombs of their relatives during the night, sung, drank and danced; according to some scholars the scenes could sometimes even be "orgiastic",[106] because *"the frontier between death and life disappears with the feast and the inebriation, the border that separates the living world and the Hereafter*

← Fig. 13
Dancing women on the left making the nwn gesture in the Festival of the Valley. Relief from the Red Chapel of Hatshepsut. Thebes. Dynasty XVIII. Temple of Karnak, Open Air Museum. Photo: María Rosa Valdesogo.

becomes blurred during the course of the night."[107]
In the New Kingdom the last visit of Amon in his procession was to the sanctuary of Queen Hatshepsut in her temple at Deir el-Bahari,[108] where the image of the god spent many days and nights. During the last night the encounter between Amon and Hathor, the Cow Goddess, took place. The sacred barque was circled by torches over the "golden lake" (*š n nbw*), which was surrounded by four ponds full of milk. The morning after, those torches were put out in the milk. According to the scholar Naguib, the milk in the ponds symbolized the milk of the Sacred Cow, the nourishment of Hathor. At the same time these four ponds symbolized the four cardinal points. So, *"the solar God enters the belly of the cosmic mother for renewal thanks to her milk, the same milk in which the fire of the night is put out"*.[109] After that night, the procession returned to the temple of Karnak. As a consequence of this encounter, Amon was reenergized and ready for facing a new year. In fact, it was a funerary festivity in which the god, as if he was dead, made a trip to the necropolis and was renewed after some ceremonial practices (the principle is the same one as in the Sed Festival). The Festival of the Valley took place before the inundation, and during that night of ecstasy Hathor showed her most erotic side. She was *"the lady of the inebriation, the happiness in ecstasy, she promoted abundance and fertility"*[110] in whose night the inundation was conceived.[111] The feminine being (Hathor) awarded the masculine principle (Amon) the power of fecundity, confirming this way the enthronement of the solar god.

Back at Deir el-Bahari in the sanctuary of the temple of Hatshepsut there is a scene of the solar barque in procession. In it two kneeling women are touching their napes and covering their faces with their hair (fig. 14). And in the tomb of Amenemhat (TT 53) from

105 Naguib, 1990. Leuven, p.129.
106 Stadelmann, 1990, p.148.
107 Stadelmann, 1990, p.149.
108 Naguib, 1990, p.126.
109 Naguib, 1990, p.128.
110 Naguib, 1990, p.129.
111 Naguib, 1990, p.130.

the reign of Tutmosis III (New Kingdom) there is a very similar scene; some women are dancing or tumbling, and they cover their faces with their hair. In front of them three more women are shaking *sistrums* and a *mena* necklace. So, this ceremony was related to the cult of Hathor. In the 1930s, E. Brunner-Traut already compared the women who appear in the Red Chapel of Hatshepsut to the mourners in the tombs of Renni and Amenemhat, but she assumed that they had nothing to do with each other.[112] According to her, the dancers of the Red Chapel were making a gesture of excitement and ecstasy,[113] while the movements of the mourners were just a part of the moan.[114] However, H. Wild suggested that the texts in Chapters 1005 and 1974 of the *Pyramid Texts* about mourners pulling hair *("The souls of Buto rock for you; they beat their bodies and their arms for you, they pull their hair for you...")* was a description of a special dance in honor of the deceased king.[115] In the 1970s J. Vandier suggested that these movements were acrobatic dances and that these women were making somersaults;[116] the kneeling women would be waiting their turn for doing the same exercise as their fellow dancers.[117] He pointed to the fact that the women were not in a vertical position, so maybe they were ready for making the somersault backwards.[118] In the 1980s W. Decker, based on a reconstruction made by O. Keel,[119] accepted Vandier's theory and thought that the women with the hair over their faces were in fact getting ready for the somersault forwards.[120] W. Decker also compared this gesture to the one made by mourners in funerals (in particular with a mourner in the Tomb of Minakht). However, it seems unlikely that they describe similar moments, since in the first document they are among a group of dancing women, and in the tomb of Minakht the mourner is alone.

→ Fig. 14
Kneeling women on the left making the nwn gesture during the procession in the Festival of the Valley. Relief from the sanctuary of the temple of Hatshepsut in Deir el-Bahari. Thebes. Dynasty XVIII. Photo: María Rosa Valdesogo.

It seems evident that those women were performing some sort of acrobatics, but it is difficult to believe that covering their faces with their hair was just a way of representing the first step of a somersault. The gesture *nwn* in the images of the dancers at the Festival of the Valley is not realistic at all. If we think of a gymnast gaining momentum, the hair is never covering the face (although realism in Egyptian art is subject of debate of course). However, taking into consideration that, in tombs as well as in temples, we see

112 Brunner-Traut, 1938, p.51, n. 13.
113 Brunner-Traut, 1938, p.52.
114 Brunner-Traut, 1938, p.60.
115 Wild, 1963, p.86.
116 Vandier, 1964, p.451.
117 Vandier, 1964, p.450.
118 Vandier, 1964, p.450.
119 Keel, 1974, fig.11
120 Decker, 1987, pp.140-142.

ceremonies with an intention to regenerate, it is likely that the *nwn* gesture in the Festival of the Valley had a reviving purpose. Dancers and mourners make the same movement of bending the body and throwing the hair forwards, and in both cases this gesture apparently has similar symbolism. Furthermore, dancing is very common in religious rituals[121] and has a connection to lunar rites.[122] *"The dance is considered beneficial magic for promoting the lunar rebirth."*[123] If we take into account that the Festival of the Valley was a funerary ceremony celebrated after the first new moon (a symbol of death) and before the flood (the annual rejuvenation in Egypt), we can draw the conclusion that it was, as in burials, a new creation rite, it was the announcement of a cyclic rejuvenation and the reenergizing of Amon.[124]

2.2 Hair as a symbol of chaos

If, in the Egyptian belief, hair is associated with the primordial waters of *Nun*, we could also consider a connection with the concept of chaos. The mourner shakes her hair while she is crying, weeping and regretting death. The weeping and the mourning happen when there is disorder. In the Osiris myth, when the god died, the world without a ruler, was in a great chaos; the death of Osiris meant confusion, darkness and disaster. In this context we could assume that the *nwn* gesture of shaking the hair forwards and covering the face with it symbolizes the chaos and darkness caused by death; mourners hide their faces and cannot see, in the same manner Osiris is blind because he is dead. Because death and lack of visibility go together and death is triumphed through the head: the lack of a head logically signifies a lack of life, since it is impossible to see and breathe without a head. The hair over the face is therefore a gesture with a deep symbolic meaning. It plunges the mourner into the same blindness as the deceased. Consequently, moving that hair away from the face allows the mourner to see and to pass from the shadows of death to the brightness of resurrection.

In Ancient Egypt, death was not considered to be the end of a human being. Dying was part of life itself. A dead person did not disappear, but was transformed. Dying was another step in the life cycle, similar to other natural events: lunar and solar cycles, the annual flood, the vegetation cycle, etc. The burial was therefore only a transition, through which the dead person was changing his condition. At funerals, mourning women would cover their faces with their hair to reproduce the shadow in which the deceased was now; at the moment of resurrection they would uncover their faces, recreating in this way the return to light. Chaos is a *"personification of the primitive vacuum, before the creation"*[125] and it is necessary to return to it in order to find the first manifestation of life.

---

121 *"Funerary dances take part in rites of passage, as in breaking rites of African cultures"* (Naguib, 1993, p.29).

122 Briffault, 1974, p.341.

123 Briffault, 1974, p.342.

124 The physical activity (the movement) is an aid for resurrection. Amon, as the king of gods, had to renew his power, as in the living world did the pharaoh.

125 Chevalier et Gheerbrandt, 1969, p.325.

In the funerary context it culminates with the resurrection of the dead. Death is a return to the first moment of creation, and in this revitalizing act of new creation the life-giving gesture of shaking the hair was crucial to the deceased.

2.3 Hair as a symbol of vegetation

If tears could be associated with water and the inundation,[126] could we then consider hair to be the banks of the Nile and its vegetation? If so, we would have a very symbolic image of Egypt: the tears dropping from the eyes would be the Nile, while the hair framing the face would be the two banks of the river (fig. 15). At that point, the fact that an Egyptian word for "*vegetation*" was *šn-tꜣ*[127]: *"the hair of the earth"*, becomes relevant. Egyptian funerary texts from the Middle Kingdom also compare both banks of the river to the manes *šnw* of Isis and Nephthys: *"Join both banks. The hair of Isis is tied to the hair of Nephthys (and) vice versa (ṯs šnw n ꜣst n šnw n Nbt-ḥwt ṯs pẖr)*[128]*...fluids*[129] *have no boat. The river is dry. Geb has taken the water up. Both hands of Smsw are united over the lungs of The Two Ladies."*[130]

→ Fig. 15
Mourning women with teardrops from their eyes. Detail from the tomb of Ramose (TT55). Thebes. Dynasty XVIII. Photo: María Rosa Valdesogo.

Like 'to unite both manes of hair', *šnw* also means to join both banks together, and this would allow the dead to pass to the Hereafter without needing any boat. The hair of Isis and Nephthys was a means of achieving resurrection: *"The hair of Isis is united to the mane of Nephthys.... The west bank joins the east bank. Both unite when they were separated before. Then I passed across...I am reunited with both sisters, they do not suffer anymore...."*[131] The union of both shores symbolized the reconciliation of the two sisters. According to one version of the myth, Osiris committed adultery with Isis's sister Nephthys, from which Anubis was born. Obviously, that caused discord between both sisters. In the symbolic dimension the union of both manes was the end of this discord, as we can read in *Book of the Dead*: "*Pray to Osiris... both shores are reconciled... he has caught aversion from their hearts for you, they hug each other*".[132]

To this matter Papyrus Salt 825 in the British Museum dating to the Late Period is also relevant. It contains the rites to preserve life[133] which were performed during the month

126 *Vide supra* p.27.

127 

128 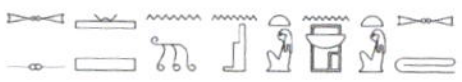

129 Referring to the putrefied Osiris corpse.

130 *CT* 168.

131 *CT* 562.

132 *BD*, 183.

133 Derchain, 1964.

of Thot[134], and the texts reads: (I,1) *"The night is not lighter135 and the day does not exist.136 One mourning is made twice in the sky and on the earth (I,2) Gods and goddesses put their hands over their heads, the earth is devastated (I,3) the sun does not rise and the moon is late, it does not exist. The Nun staggers; (I,4) the earth frets; the river is not navigable anymore. (I,5)...Listen. Everybody is moaning and crying. The souls, (I,6) the gods, the goddesses, people, the Axw, the dead ones, small animals (I,7) and big ones, the... cry, cry so much,....."[137]* The importance of this passage lies in the writing of the expression *"the earth is devastated"*: *iw tꜣ fk.* The verb *fk* is the same as *fꜣk*, which means *"to be bald"*.[138] The waste-

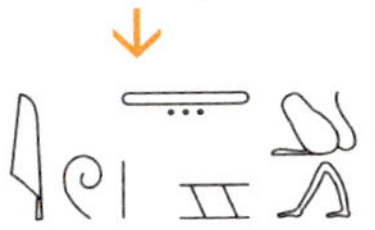

land is an earth without hair. If the absence of hair is a parallel of the absence of plants,[139] the hair *šnw* of Isis and Nepthys could easily be assimilated to the vegetation.

Life and death in Ancient Egypt were vital to nature and the seasons. The inundation spread the mud all over the land, fertilized it and made it possible for the vegetation to grow once the water had retired. This happened during *prt*, the season of sowing. Where the hair element was previously related to water, it is now linked to plants as the result of the fertilization of the land, thanks to the regenerating waters. It is also interesting to point out that in Chapter 167 of the *Coffin Texts* the mourners give their hair, *smꜣ*, while in the following Chapter 168 the hair, *šnw*, of Isis and Nephthys gets tied, so we might wonder if we are dealing with two successive acts or if the *nwn* gesture could mean two different things.

The funerary cult is usually influenced by the cult of fertility and the *"sacrifices and/ or offerings to the ancestral souls are taken from agricultural rites"*.[140] The Osiris rite is an agricultural and lunar ritual, where lunar cycle and agrarian rites are mixed. Just like the moon, plants also have a cycle of birth, growing, death and resurrection[141] and for that reason the lunar divinities are also vegetation gods in Egyptian religion. The Egyptian year started with the flooding of the Nile and the first month of the first season (*ꜣḫt*)[142] was called *tḫi*, which meant *"inebriation"*. Inebriation and inundation together make us think of concepts such as chaos and orgy and also of the disorder of the hair, *smꜣ*, since the verb *tḫtḫ* (duplication de *tḫi*) means *"to dishevel"*.[143]

---

134   When the ceremony took place there were also some other funerary festivities (Derchain, 1964, p.63).

135   The moonlight does not illuminate.

136   Darkness caused by the death.

137   Derchain, 1964, p.137.

138   *Wb* I, 579.

139   Among agricultural people the growing of hair is linked to the image of the growing of alimentary plants, and the idea of growing up is related to the idea of rise. (Chevalier et Gheerbrandt, 1969, p.369).

140   Elíade, 1970, p.297.

141   The seasons are also cyclic (from drought to fertility).

142   In Ancient Egypt there were three seasons: *ꜣḫt* (inundation), *prt* (sowing) and *šmw* (harvest).

143   *Wb* V, 328, 8.

PART II | Shaking and Pulling hair

In the month of *Khoiak*, at the end of the first season, the festival for Osiris took place. The mutilated god came back to life in the shape of the moon and in the shape of a plant. Both are perfect images of resurrection. In those rites, grains were put into moulds in the shape of the mummy of Osiris, where those grains would grow into plants. On the 23rd of that month, a ceremony symbolizing the search for and collection of the pieces of the corpse of Osiris, and the embalming executed by Anubis in the *Golden House* (*ḥwt-nbw*) took place. According to some documents of the Middle and New Kingdom, the 23rd day of the *Khoiak* month was also called the day of the "*Great Mourning*" (*Prt-ꜥꜣt*), so it was assumed that on that day Isis and Nephthys were performing their official mourning for the death of Osiris. In the night of the 25th, the *Lamentations of Isis and Nephthys* took place, and songs were read aloud by two women representing the two goddesses. Just after that mourning rite, at sunrise on the 26th, the resurrection of Osiris took place. In conclusion, the first season of the Egyptian year (*ꜣḫt*) started with the inebriation (*tḫi*), the disorder, the chaos and the primeval waters of the flood, and finished with the fertilization of the land, the end of the darkness and the resurrection of Osiris after a mourning rite (*Prt-ꜥꜣt*), performed by Isis and Nephthys. The hair of Isis and Nepthys therefore played a role related to the life cycle: first the *smꜣ* was associated with water, the inundation, the *Nun*, as a receptacle of regenerating principles, afterwards the hair, *šnw*, was connected with vegetation, as the product of creation and as a manifestation of life. This would also explain the succession of Chapters 167 and 168 in the *Coffin Texts*. Once again hair is an element related to life. Although we have now seen two different terms, first *smꜣ* and then *šnw*, we are not leaving the funerary and mourning context. The verb *šni* means "*to suffer*"[144] and is the root of the name of *šntꜣyt*.[145] This goddess, who is documented from Dynasty XIX onwards, was associated with Isis as a mourner and the widow of Osiris and appears in funerary rites of regeneration and purification of this god.[146]

3. The symbolism of shaking the hair forwards in Ancient Egyptian belief

3.1. The Hair Gives the Breath of Life

Breathing is essential for living and also for rebirth. On the rocky island of Bigeh, near Philae, the sanctuary of Abaton was located[147] dedicated to the god Osiris. It was also considered the tomb of this god. Here, Isis and Nephthys moaned[148] and "*Osiris received the crying from your mouth and his soul breathes thanks to the weeping*".[149] So breath can be transmitted to the dead by means of mourning. In the Chapter 228 of the *Coffin Texts* the breath of the deceased is assured thanks to different aspects of hair, because the

144 *Wb* IV, 494

145 *Wb* IV, 518, 3.

146 Cauville, 1981, pp.21-40.

147 This word is derived from a Greek word and translates as the "forbidden place", because only priests were allowed in.

148 Guglielmi, 1980, p.81.

149 Guglielmi, 1980, p.80.

dead *"breathes the east wind through her plait, he catches the north wind through her plait, he takes the south wind through his plaits,*[150] *he takes the west wind through his curls (or his plaits)....*"[151] Thanks to the hair element the dead or Osiris can breathe the wind from the four cardinal points,[152] in the same way that he could breathe in Abaton thanks to the weeping of Isis and Nephthys.

Again, hair and mourning are two inseparable aspects and once again this combination hair-mourning-breath leads us to the Osiris Myth, in particular when Isis as a kite flapped her wings over the corpse of Osiris and the created air caused his resurrection. Furthermore, it is also interesting to have a look at the word *ḥw*, which indicates a movement made by feathers and is written with the hair determinative;[153] also words such as "*feather*" (*šwt*)[154] or "*wings*" (*ḏnḥw*)[155] could be written with the hair determinative in some cases. The combination feather-kite-air seems to be closely linked to the combination hair-mourning-breath; it would not be far-fetched to assume a relationship between the kite's feather (in the mythical dimension) and the mourner's hair (in the ritual dimension), both elements creating the breath of life.

← Fig. 16
Stele of Lady Taperet. Thebes? Dynasty XXII. Paris, Musée du Louvre, E52. Photo: ©RMN-Grand Palais.

150 On some coffins we read "*eyebrow*".

151 A very similar passage is in the *Book of the Dead* (*LdM* 172).

152 In the *Coffin Texts* we read: "*...the hands of šsmw are united over the lungs...*" (*CT* III, 168); and in coffin B4Bo the writing for "lungs" is 

153  *CT* II, 148

154 

155 

3.2. Shaking the hair is maternity in Egyptian funerary thought

If death was a return to the first moment of creation, the deceased - as a human being - also had to return to that first moment of a person: birth. This birth had three mythical dimensions in the Egyptian belief:

1. Already in the Old Kingdom Isis and Nephthys were considered responsible for the resurrection of the dead (or rebirth): *"Unas goes up through the two thighs of Isis. Unas rises through the two thighs of Nepthys".*[156] Both goddesses were the two women who conceived and who gave birth to the Pharaoh, and the latter rose to heaven after his night travel (thus his death).

2. In the funerary context, the dead, assimilated to Osiris, had to be reborn as the son of Geb and Nut: *"he is the first-born of Geb, the first-born son of Nut, the one who goes out from the womb with the uraeus."*[157]

3. The resurrection of the deceased was also of a lunar nature because in another explanation of the lunar cycle, this celestial body was born from the womb of the sky goddess Nut and was then swallowed by her at the end of the cycle.[158]

Considering these three points, we may assume that in Egyptian funerals the two women representing Isis and Nephthys gave birth to the new-born (the dead) and somehow also took on the role of mothers for the deceased in the symbolic sphere. We read in the *Pyramid Texts* that "*Isis has conceived him and Nephthys has nursed him.*"[159] The funerary texts in the Old Kingdom already show a connection between the goddess Nut and hair in the context of rebirth: "*Nut gives you her two arms, she with the long hair, whose breasts are suspended (dỉ.n Nwt ꜥwy.s ỉr.k ꜣwt šny sẖdẖdt mnḏy).*"[160] Later we read that the deceased "*...goes up to Busiris to see Osiris...*" and "*Nut shakes her hair when she sees me....*"[161] From these quotes we imagine the goddess Nut making the *nwn* gesture of shaking her hair forwards when she receives her son Osiris. This image of Nut provided by religious texts also has an iconographical basis. The funerary stele of the Lady Taperet from Dynasty XXII [162] is a small wooden stele with painted decoration on both sides. On one side, Taperet prays to the falcon-headed god Re-Horakhty and on the other side she prays to the god Atum. On both sides the upper part is decorated with the vault of heaven. In the image where Taperet prays to Atum the whole perimeter is occupied by the goddess Nut as the firmament: she bends her body and her hair falls down (fig. 16). The artists captured how Nut swallowed the moon, which is regenerated inside her starry body to be reborn from her womb. There is a similar example on a relief in the coffin

156 *Pyr.*, 379c and 996c.

157 Mariette, 1875, 152-153, 3; Derchain, 1963, p.22.

158 Derchain, 1962, p.27.

159 *Pyr.* 1154.

160  *Pyr.* 2171 a.

161 *CT* I, 312 and *BD* 78.

162 The Louvre Museum, E52

of Uresh-Unefer from Dynasty XXX ,[163] which has a depiction of Nut bending down and with a suspended lock of hair.

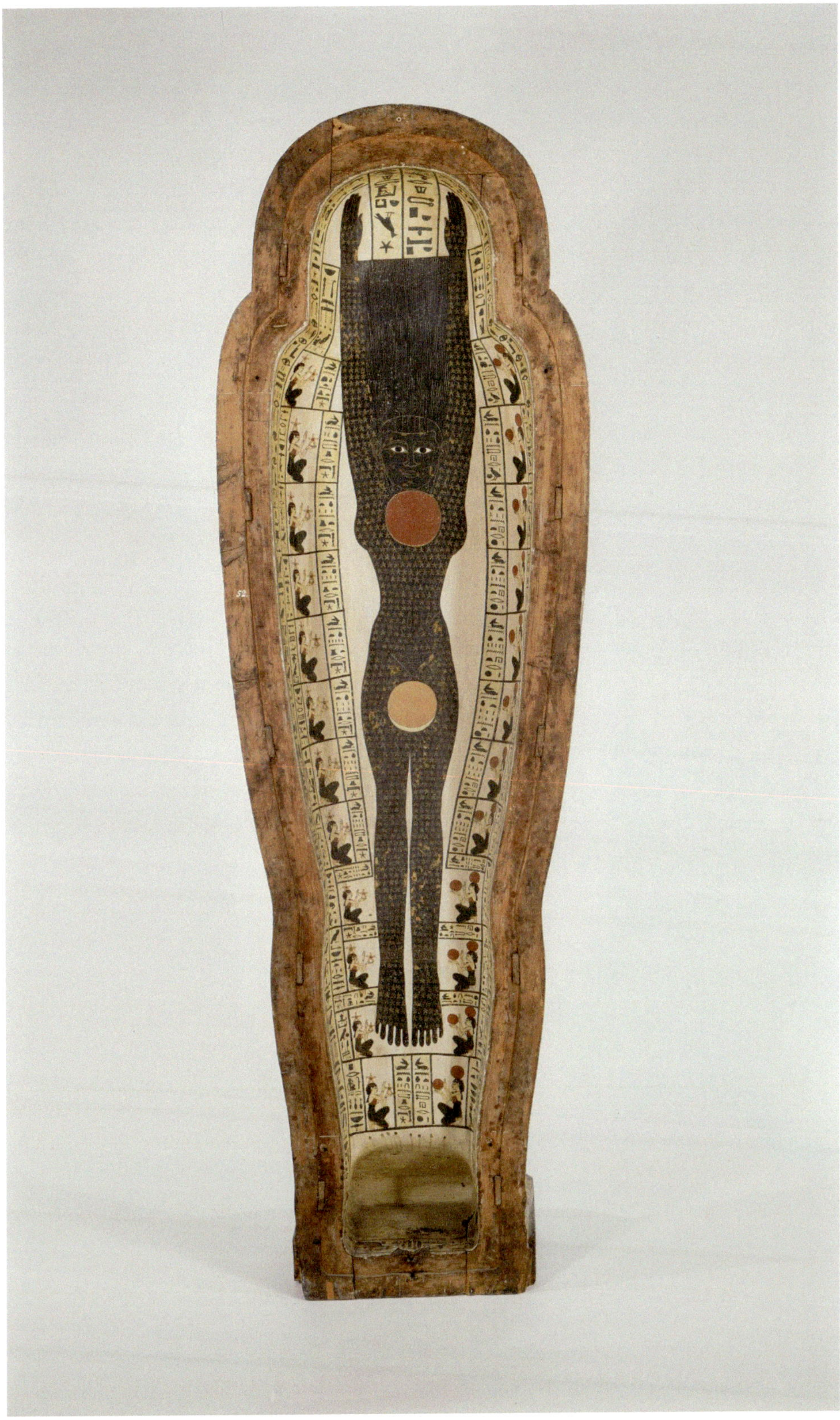

← Fig. 17
Image of Nut on the internal side of the cover in the coffin of Peftjau-neith. Dynasty XXVI. Leiden, Rijksmuseum van Oudheden, AMM 5-e. Photo: ©National Museum of Antiquities, Leiden, The Netherlands.

163 Metropolitan Museum of Art of New York, inv. No. 14.7.1

This image of Nut and the fact that she is the mother of Osiris in Ancient Egyptian cosmogony may lead us to the conclusion that passages from the *Pyramid Texts*, *Coffin Texts* and *Book of the Dead* allude to the birth of the dead. Nut, bended and with her face looking at her pubis observes how her son (the dead) is coming to life. This also relates to textual evidence that Nut shakes her hair when she sees Osiris, because in that moment she is making the *nwn* gesture. This posture has a very strong symbolic meaning: it is an image of maternity and closely related to the rebirth of Osiris.

There are many examples of coffins from the Late Period with representations of Nut on the inner side of the lid. On them, the goddess is frontally extended over the whole surface with her mane of hair standing upright (fig. 17). In this case we see a different perspective of the same posture. On this lid, Nut would also be making the *nwn* gesture of shaking the hair forwards. The goddess, as the sky vault, swallows the evening sun and gives birth to the morning sun. Several times Nut is the night sky, so she swallows the evening sun and gives birth to the full moon. The coffin in Ancient Egypt is not just the receptacle of the mummy; on its interior the conception and rebirth of the dead take place. Nut bended and with her hair falling down, gives birth to her son Osiris and puts her arms around him: "*...Geb is there protecting you; he is your father, you have been put on the world by him; the arms of Nut are around you, she has brought you to life, she brings your beauty....*"[164]

→ **Fig. 18**
Scene of a feminine figure bending over the dead. Coffin of Henui from Gebelein. Dynasty XIII (After Steindorff. *Grabfunde des Mittleren Reichs in den Königlichen Museen zu Berlin*, Berlin, 1901, p. 13)

Summed up, the *nwn* gesture of shaking the hair forwards made by mourners in Ancient Egypt would symbolize the first moment in the life of a human being. Women reproduced the gesture made by the goddess Nut when she gave birth to her son Osiris. So, when the mourners shook their hair forwards at funerals, they would contribute to the rebirth of the deceased.

3.3 Shaking the hair symbolizes having sex in Egyptian funerary thought

We already know the relationship between mourning and hair and its connection to the Osiris legend. A very important part of that myth is the episode where Osiris recovers his virility. According to the legend, once the different parts of Osiris's corpse were found and the body was restored, Isis placed herself over her husband's body and conceived Horus, his posthumous son. Thanks to that act, the cosmic order was re-established; Horus became the king of Egypt and Osiris was resurrected as the king of the Hereafter.

---

164 *CT* I, 60. Translated by Barguet, 1986, p.198.

← **Fig. 19**
Stele of Sebekaa. Dynasty XI. Thebes. London, British Museum, EA1372. Photo: © The Trustees of the British Museum.

On the coffin of Henui found in Gebelein dating to Dynasty XIII ,[165] there is a scene with two women assisting the dead and a female figure is bending over him (fig. 18). The stele of Sebekaa, from Thebes dating to Dynasty XI[166] contains a number of funerary scenes; among them there is one that shows the deceased on the bier being embraced by a figure on top of him (fig. 19). Already in the 1950s Chr. Desroches-Noblecourt considered that the aim of this gesture was to return virility to the mummy.[167] Further, the *Pyramid Texts* show that in the Old Kingdom Isis and Nephthys were considered responsible for regenerating the deceased's potential for procreation.[168] Additionally, Egyptian iconography has several examples of the copulation of Isis and Osiris. Isis as a kite[169] places herself over the phallus of her husband (fig. 20). In this way she assures the conception of Horus. He will be the son who will avenge the murder of his father. We can also find many examples of this in the literature:

"I am your sister Isis. No god and no goddess have done what I have done. I have performed the procreation, although I am a woman alone, for making your name to endure on earth. Your divine semen was inside my womb and I put it over the earth, this way he can spread your image. He is healthy, although you suffer. He must send the violence to those who had caused it. Seth succumb to his knife. Fellows of Seth succumb because of Seth. The throne of Geb is yours. You are his beloved son...."[170]

The Songs of Isis and Nephthys state that the two women who represented Isis and Nephthys in the Osiris festivals "*should not have been opened*" *(nn wp(t).sn)*. I would like to discuss the meaning of this sentence here. The verb *wpỉ* means "*to separate*" or "*to open*"[171] and according to R.O. Faulkner this expression meant that the two mourners representing Isis and Nephthys should be virgins. However, the verb *wpi* relates to the concept of maternity, because a non-opened body or belly refers to a body that has not yet given

165 Berlin Museum 13772

166 British Museum EA1372

167 Desroches-Noblecourt, 1953, p.43.

168 *Pyr.*, 366, 628 a, 631 b, 632 a-d and 123-125.

169 Roeder, 1960, p.180.

170 Pap. Louvre, 3079; Roeder, 1960, p.182.

171 *Wb* I, 298.

birth.[172] The Egyptian expression "*they have not been opened with birth*" (*n wpt.sn m mst*)[173] that should be considered here means: 'they have not yet given birth and have not been a mother yet'. Further, in those texts Osiris is "*the first-born who opens the body*".[174] So maybe we should assume that one of the requirements for being a mourner in the role of Isis and Nephthys was not to be a mother yet, and to have the ability of conceiving intact. This was a way of being faithful to the myth and also a way of securing the resurrection

→ Fig. 20
Isis as a kite over the body of the dead. Statuette of prince Tutmosis, son of Amenhotep III. Dynasty XVIII. Thebes. Berlin, Neues Museum. Photo: María Rosa Valdesogo.

of the dead, because the conceiving faculty of both Isis and Nephthys was untouched.[175]

The Songs of Isis and Nephthys tell how, after the chaos and disaster caused by Seth when killing Osiris, the resurrection comes when *"the one who is removed, is removed from death. Our eyes cry over you..."*[176]; and how the two mourners cry: "*Be powerful thanks to us and to the moan(?). They join your body for you while mourning*".[177] The revitalizing power of the tears and moaning helps in lifting Osiris from death. This exhilarating aspect of lament is also evident in the *Harper's Song* in the tomb of Intef.[178] It is a very pessimistic poem affirming that death is the end of everything and nobody can do anything to avoid

172 *Wb* I, 300, 8.

173 Pap. Westcar 5, 11.

174 *Songs*...1, 19; 1, 24; 8, 25; 9, 15 and 9, 17.

175 Ph. Derchain also considered that it meant two childless women (Derchain, 1975, p.73). It is also interesting to note that in the myth of Osiris Isis has not yet given birth to Horus. He is born after his father's death and his birth is the guarantee of the resurrection of Osiris. So, in the funerary ceremony the idea would be the same: maternity happens after death.

176 *Songs*...3, 2.

177 *Songs*..11, 6-7.

178 Fox, 1977, pp.393-423. Lichtheim, 1973, pp.194-197. This poem was in his tomb, dating to the year 2.100 b. C. The text was preserved in two copies from the New Kingdom: Pap. British Museum 10060 and the tomb of Paatenemheb in Saqqara (the latter from the reign of Akhenaton).

it. For that reason it is also very sceptic about the effectiveness of the funerary ceremonies for the resurrection of the dead: *"It is the day for the cries of mourning. Their*[179] *moans cannot save from the Afterlife a man's heart..."* Although it is quite negative, this premise confirms the fact that there was a mourning rite in Ancient Egypt for helping the dead to return to life. The evidence for the existence of such a mourning rite is the fact that Isis and Nephthys were mourners, shook their hair and contributed to the resurrection of the deceased; according to the sacred texts, one of the main responsibilities was the conception of Osiris's son by Isis.

At this point, I have to mention the female figurines found in some tombs of the Middle Kingdom, which may have been used for restoring virility to the dead.[180] According to Chr. Desroches-Noblecourt, these figurines showed no visible effects of maternity, so they could symbolize young femininity. They would not be images of fecundity, but of eroticism.[181] That premise would lead us back to our previous idea: the two mourners in the roles of Isis and Nephthys should not be mothers yet.

In Egyptian thought the dead had a sexual aspect because he was "*the one who ejaculates over the mourners*"[182] and Osiris is "*the lord of the sexual pleasure*" (*nb nḏmnḏm*),[183] "*the lord of the love*" (*nb mrwt*)[184] and *"the bull that fertilizes the cows"* (*kꜣ st m ḥmwt*).[185] Osiris is also the one who "*gives life to the woman*",[186] i.e. who "*impregnates her*". For that reason he is called "*the one who begets*"[187] and the mourners ask him to have sexual relations saying: *"Copulate you with us as a male" (smꜣ.k im.n mi ṯꜣy),*[188] *"Copulate you with your sister Isis" (ꜣpd.k sn(t).k ꜣst).*[189] It is important in that aspect to mention one scene of resurrection in the tomb of Petosiris. The deceased, assimilated with Osiris and represented as a scarab with the *atef* crown, has the goddess Isis on both sides. The Isis on the right is represented with the sign of the full sail, symbol of breath and wind. In this scene the goddess is called the Lady of the North, the Lady of vivifying wind, while Osiris is copulating: "*Words said by Isis, Lady of the red crown: the north wind is destined to your nose... I made your throat breathe. The divine mother, she joined the limbs of her brother in the palace. They look for Osiris... he is in copulation.*" [190]

---

179 The mourners.

180 It looks as if these figurines were also put in tombs of the New Kingdom for restoring the *ka* of the dead (Desroches-Noblecourt, 1953 p.39).

181 Desroches-Noblecourt, 1953, p.18. However, she accepts the idea of the virginity of the two mourners representing Isis and Nephthys.

182 *CT* 991. *Vide supra* p.22.

183 *Songs*...1,23; 12,8.

184 *Songs*...3,5.

185 *Songs*...3,6.

186 *Songs*...14,27.

187 *Songs*...3,26.

188 *Songs*...2,9.

189 *Songs*...5,25.

190 Daumas, 1960, p.68, pl.I.

There is a very important sequence in *The Songs of Isis and Nephthys* related to the sexual moment: *"Lord of the sexual pleasure, Oh! Come to me; be in union the sky and the earth."*[191] In the mythic sphere the primeval union is the one between earth and sky. In Egyptian cosmogony the copulation between Geb and Nut is the moment of creation, symbolized by the sexual act, which contains the power of generating life. In Egyptian iconography this primeval moment is depicted with the image of Nut bending her body over Geb, who lies face up on the ground waiting for her (fig. 21). It is the union of the masculine principle with feminine principle, the Hierogamy, which provokes the first manifestation of life.

→ Fig. 21
Nut bending over Geb (After Budget, *The Gods of the Egyptians*, Chicago, 1904)

In many cultures sex is something closely related to agricultural fecundity; it is an act in favour of life to stimulate new births; and there is also a link between vegetation and eroticism. According to M. Eliade "*moments of cosmic crisis are a pretext for the unleashing of an orgy. The earth needs to be revived and the sky needs to be excited, to create good conditions for the cosmic Hierogamy; this way grain grows, women bear children, animals reproduce and dead ones fill their vacuum with vital power.*"[192] Therefore, the orgy is a renovating act and it is a way of repeating creation, because it reproduces the chaos of the primeval moment,[193] from which the new order emerges. Orgy is the image of chaos. Orgiastic festivities allude to the chaotic moment in which the world is lost and from where the new power arises to reorganize and restore the cosmic order. As J. E. Cirlot says: "*the goal is not to obtain physical pleasure, but to help the world dissoluteness; a temporary breaking-off for the following restoration of the original 'illud tempus'.*"[194] An orgy is an act that generates life.

The orgy also has a connection with the moon, since the moon regenerates itself monthly after a moment of chaos and darkness. The moon is also the light-giving celestial

191 *Songs*...12, 8-9-10. There are further allusions to that matter in lines 7, 4; 12, 11-12; 12, 16.

192 Eliade, 1970, p.301.

193 Durand, 1979, p.297

194 Cirlot, 1991, p.341.

body of the night, when shadow reigns. And the moon is related to vegetation, since the agrarian rites are also lunar rituals with a strong regenerative nature. In fact, it is common from prehistoric times onwards to find lunar symbols with erotic connotations. For instance, the spiral as a geometrical sign was a lunar symbol, because it derives from the snail's shell, an animal that appears and disappears, like the moon, and there was an analogy between the shell and the vulva.[195]All this could be combined in the Egyptian funerary context with the figure of Osiris (since he was a lunar god) a god of vegetation and the Osiris myth had many erotic connotations. Obviously, I am not implying that during Egyptian funerals orgiastic practices took place, but there was a sexual symbolism in some funerary practices and their final goals were the resurrection of the deceased. It seems rather logical to think that the *nwn* gesture made by the two mourners in the role of Isis and Nephthys had a sexual nature and was crucial for the mummy's new life. As R. Briffault says: "*the reproduction through the sexual act could be considered, according to primitive thought, as an alternative to eternal life.*"[196] Sex means fecundity and birth, and rebirth in the funerary belief.

In this regard, I would like to mention Chapter 17 of the *Book of the Dead*, which captures perfectly all we have been discussing:[197]

"*I am Isis, you found me when*[198] *I had my hair in disorder*[199] *over my face, and my crown*[200] *was dishevelled.*[201] *I have conceived*[202] *as Isis, I have procreated as Nephthys. Isis dispels my*

195 Elíade, 1970, p.140.

196 Briffault, 1974, p.313.

197 *Urk.*V, 87, 1-7; *Urk.* V, 89, 1-3.

198 *sḏm.n.f* expressing past tense.

199 The verb *psḫ* can be transitive: "*to dishevel the hair*" or intransitive: "*to be crazy*", "*to despair*". It could also refer to the disorder of the hair or of the heart because of fear (*Wb* I, 550, 16).

200 *Wpt* can be translated as "*crown*" or the "*top of the head*". *Rꜣ* can be "*the beginning*", as point of origin at the scalp, where the hair starts, so the "*crown*"; or also the beginning of the hair at the face, so the forehead.

201 The verb *tḫtḫ* means "*to dishevel the hair*" (*Wb* V, 328, 8).

202 The verb *ỉwr* means "*to conceive*", "*to be pregnant*" (*Wb* I, 56, 1).

bothers (?).[203] *My crown is dishevelled; Isis has been above her secret, she has stood up*[204] *and has cleaned*[205] *her hair."*[206]

H. Goedicke states that the chapter clearly describes the copulation of Isis and Osiris.[207] Isis, making the *nwn* gesture, places herself over the body of her husband Osiris, who lies face up (it recalls the Hierogamy and the image of Nut and Geb); she gets pregnant and protects the dead. All these actions are the goddess' secret; afterwards Isis stands up and rearranges her hair.[208] Isis had to assure a descendant of the deceased, because the earth needed an heir for the throne, who also had to help in his father's resurrection. Therefore, Isis as a kite landed on top of her husband, she flapped her wings to give him the breath of life and placed herself on top of his phallus to return his virility to him and conceive Horus. The birth of the son means the victory over temporality by means of perpetuating the lineage; because the second element is the result and reflection of the previous one.[209] The son becomes the image of eternity and balance in the same person. And this process led by Isis "*is something that needs to be hidden, it is not allowed that a man or a woman divulges it*".[210] Maybe that is the reason why the act is described as a secret and could also explain the scarcity of documents describing it.

Furthermore, the verb "*to dishevel the hair*" (*tḫtḫ*) has the same root as "*inebriation*" (*tḫi*). According to A. Gutbub, the feat of inebriation in honor of Hathor, which was a part of the Festival of the Valley, was perhaps also celebrated in funerals in honour of the deceased.[211] And regarding the Sed Festival, this scholar considers that the ritual *wpi ḥn,* made during that celebration, can be interpreted as the union of Hathor with the king during a drunken celebration.[212] That being the case, this sexual element could be part of rejuvenating rites. The aim of these rituals was to change of status of the person who is the subject of the ceremony, by means of returning to the primeval moment and the subsequent rebirth. It makes sense to consider the *nwn* gesture of shaking the hair forwards made in funerals by the two 'professional mourners' representing Isis and

---

203 According to Erman and Grapow, *sȝwt* means "*safe-keeping*" (*Wb* III, 418, 5); but if we apply this translation, the sentence makes no sense. In another version of chapter 17 of the *Book of the Dead*, with *ḏr.s sȝwt.i*, we read: *Nb-ḥwt bḫn.s ḫnnw.i* (Junker, 1917, p.157). *Bḫn* means "*to cut*" or "*to eliminate*" (*Wb* I, 468, 10; Faulkner, 1988, p.83), as a parallel with *ḏr*; and *ḫnnw* means "*disturbance*", "*disorder*" (*Wb* III, 383, 15; Faulkner, 1988, p.203), so *sȝwt* has maybe a similar meaning.

204 *ʿḥʿ.n sḏm.n.f* can be a narrative tense, so it could be translated as "*then*". But if we consider *ʿḥʿ* as a verb, the translation should be "*she stood up*".

205 The verb *sin* means "*to clean*", "*to scrub*" (*Wb* III, 425, 8; Faulkner, 1988, p.213). It would be possible to imagine Isis standing up and doing her hair after its dishevelment. (*tḫtḫ*).

206 *Urk*. V, 87, 1-4 and *Urk*. 88, 17-89, 3.

207 Goedicke, 1970, p.25. He thinks that there is also a passage in Pap. Chester Beatty I, 16, 10-11 and in Pap. Westcar 2, 1.

208 It is also interesting to point out that in Papyrus Turin, just before that episode we read: "*...both sisters are given to me for pleasure...*" (Rachewiltz, 1989, p.59).

209 Durand, 1979, p.290.

210 *Books of Breathing* cf. Desroches-Noblecourt, 1968.

211 Gutbub, 1961, p.50.

212 Gutbub, 1961, p.60.

Nephthys as a way of commemorating the sexual episode of the Osiris myth in a human version.

4. Mourning women pull their lock of hair. The *nwn m* Gesture

Egyptian reliefs and paintings show how mourners sometimes, instead of shaking the hair, pulled it as if they wanted to pull their hair out. Egyptians called this mourning gesture *nwn m* and the lock of hair was usually named swt. In the mourning scenes from the tomb of Mereruka in Saqqara and the tomb of Idu in Giza, both from Dynasty VI, women were usually depicted crying, rocking, and beating their arms and heads, but some others are pulling locks of hair from their heads.[213] This same gesture appears in the tomb of Inti in Deshasheh (near Beni Suef) from Dynasty V. However, in this case we are facing a depiction related to war, not to funerary rituals, as the city was besieged. The scene shows the mayor of the city and a woman in front of him, both are pulling a front lock of hair (fig. 22). Although it is not a mourning scene, the gesture appears in a moment of desperation and suffering, similar feelings mourners show in funerals were meant to be depicted.

← **Fig. 22**
Scene from the tomb of Inti in Deshasheh. In the second register the major and a woman pull their lock of hair. Dynasty V. Deshasheh (After Petrie, *Deshasheh*, London, 1898)

During the subsequent periods we do not find any images of common mourners pulling their hair until Dynasty XXI. On the coffin of Amenemipet,[214] found in Deir el-Bahari, there is a funerary procession scene with a group of mourning women, where one of them pulls a lateral lock of hair with both hands. Pulling hair is a mourning gesture that appears in royal documents from Dynasty XIX in the form of images of Isis and Nephthys. On the coffin set of Ramses IV, the outer coffin presents Isis and Nephthys at both sides of the head, pulling their front lock of hair. This image is accompanied by a text in which it is said that "*the two goddesses hold their swt.*" D. Meeks translated the word swt as "*lock*" or "*plait*".[215] It seems evident that, at least in this context, it describes the frontal lock of hair of both goddesses. The mourners of the Hereafter also pull their hair in the tomb of Ramses VI; and in the tomb of Ramses IX four women pull their front lock of hair while bending slightly over the mummy in a scene that originates from to the *Book of the Caverns* (fig. 23). Very similar examples are the coffins of the royal scribe

213 I would like to point to two reliefs in the tomb of Idu representing mourning men who are also pulling their hair. It is not so common to find scenes of mourning men at Ancient Egypt funerals and even less shaking their hair or pulling it. Here is maybe another subject for future research.

214 British Museum EA22941.

215 D. Meeks, 1977-1979, II, p.312, n° 78.3373.

Nes-shu-tefnut[216] and of the priest Djedhor,[217] both from Saqqara and dating to the Ptolemaic Period, in which Isis and Nephthys appear together pulling their front lock of hair. It is obvious that there is a link between pulling the lock of hair (that is the gesture *nwn m swt*) and lamenting at Egyptian funerals. For an in-depth analysis: again, the funerary texts will be the best aid, in particular the *Coffin Texts* from the Middle Kingdom.

→ Fig. 23
Scene from the tomb of Ramses IX (KV6). At the right of the top register four mourning women pull their hair over the mummy. Dynasty XX. Thebes (After Guilmant, *Tombeau de Ramses IX*, Cairo, 1907).

4.1. The lock of hair as an image of the mourner

Given the fact that all funerary rituals and funerary elements were meant to be benevolent for the deceased, it is necessary to also analyse the meaning and attributions of the funerary masks. The funerary mask in Ancient Egypt had a protective purpose. Chapter 531 of the *Coffin Texts* lists its apotropaic properties assimilating the many different parts of the mask with several divinities. After saying how perfect the face (the mask) of the dead is, the text continues: "*Your White Crown is Thoth; your crown is Wp-wꜣw.t*[218] *Your eyebrows are both Enneads. Your eyes are the boat of the day and the boat of the night. Your two locks of hair are Isis and Nephthys (swty.k m ꜣst ḥnꜥ Nbt-ḥwt)*[219]*...your nape is ¨wn-ꜥn-wy. Your plait is ¡DDt*[220] *(ḥnskt.k m ¡ḏḏt)*".[221] The dead is associated to the headless Osiris and the funerary mask is like a complete head or its substitute, and to put it over the face of the deceased is a reviving action in itself. The mask has two main functions. On the one hand it hides the damage done by Seth to Osiris's face. On the other hand it restores the capacity of the head, such as the ability to see and to breathe; and through the mask

216 Kunsthistorisches Museum in Wien 1.

217 Louvre Museum D8.

218 "*The One who opens the ways*", the name of the jackal god from Asyut, who opens the ways to the king in battle. Let us remind ourselves of its presence also in the Sed Festival.

219 

220 Scorpion Goddess, especially Isis from Edfu (*Wb* III, 206, 6). The goddess scorpion Serket was also assimilated to Isis during some period of the Egyptian history.

221 

the dead can also perceive things that mortals cannot.[222] Therefore the replacement of the head, symbolized by the placement of the mask, allows the deceased to return to life. In this context of resurrection we need to find the meaning of the mentioned locks of hair (*swty*). Due to the fact that Chapter 531 of the *Coffin Texts* describes the funerary mask, I think that this word is referring to the two locks of hair of the mask that frame the face in the same way that Isis and Nephthys are always at both ends of the dead. If the word *swt* designates the lock of hair the mourners pull, perhaps the Egyptians referred to both goddesses with the dual term *swty*, following a process of metonymy. Two locks of hair could designate Isis and Nephthys due to the relationship between them and the hair they pull. The term *ḥnskt* usually means "*plait of hair*".[223] In this chapter the two locks of hair are assimilated with Isis and Nephthys just before the text mentions the nape, so it makes sense to view *ḥnskt* as the mop of hair of the wig that falls on the back.[224] Furthermore, the Egyptian word *ḥnskty* is a dual term referring to Isis and Nephthys, which means '*the two women with plait*'.[225] And that brings us to the images of Isis and Nephthys with the headdress *ꜥfnt* or the images of mourners with the hair tied in a back tail (fig. 8); which reinforces the idea that *ḥnskt* could be the hair identified with the goddess *¡ḏḏt* (a manifestation of Isis of Edfu) in Chapter 531of the *Coffin Texts*.

In Chapter 332 of the *Coffin Texts* the deceased is guided through the darkness of death by a powerful goddess, who is "...*the lady of power, who guides those in the caverns*..." and meanwhile "...*the earth trembles because of the jubilation, while the locks of hair are in the mourning* (*sk swt m-ẖnw ỉꜣkbw*) ...."[226] The verb *sw*  means "*to be something harmful for someone*",[227] and it could maybe be translated as "*hurt* "or "*wound*". The substantive is *swt* ("*damage*", "*hurt*").[228] We can already find this verb in the *Pyramid Texts* of the Old Kingdom when they allude to the final victory of Osiris: "*The deceased is the Lord of his enemies, which have been beaten by Horus for him. Go up! Sit over him! You are stronger than him, hurt him...!*" (*dỉ ỉr.k swt ỉr.f*).[229] And in the chapters describing the typical image of the two goddesses Isis and Nephthys mourning while Anubis assists Osiris' corpse: "*Isis is sitting, her arms over her head. Nephthys, holds her breasts because of the death of her brother, Anubis is bent over his stomach, Osiris is in his damage*" (*Wsir m swt.f*).[230]

We could consider the word *swt* as a passive participle of the verb *sw*, so the translation could read: "*the damaged ones*" or "*the hurt ones*", the ones who have been damaged - that is - the mourners Isis and Nephthys; they were hurt by the death of Osiris and that

222 D. Meeks, 1991, p.7.

223 *Wb* III, 116, 4.

224 Chr. Desroches-Noblecourt considers that *ḥnsk*t refers to the small braids under the head-dress *ꜥfnt* (Chr. Desroches-Noblecourt, 1953, p.28, n.2) and that it is related to the manifestation of the ka of the deceased (Chr. Desroches-Noblecourt, 1953, p.25, n.5).

225 *Wb* III, 121, 1. It appears like that in *The Songs of Isis and Nephthys*, Pap. Bremner-Rhind I; 1,9; 3,23; 6,23 y 11,19.

226 

227 *Wb* IV, 59, 16.

228 *Wb* IV, 59, 18.

229 *Pyr.*, 652.

230 *Pyr.*, 1281-1282.

is why they are in mourning. This would also explain the frequent use of the hieroglyph of hair as a determinative for that word. We could also consider a word play with the "*locks of hair*" (*swt*) in the previous chapter, Chapter 531 of the *Coffin Texts*, and the "*hurt ones*" (*swt*) in this chapter, Chapter 332 of the *Coffin Texts*. In both cases this applies to the mourners who dishevel their hair as a sign of mourning. The "*locks of hair*" would be the "*hurt ones*", so each mourner would be identified by a lock of hair. Again, this would be a case of metonymy: the whole (the mourners) is designated using its most significant part (the hair).

The verb *sw* could also be translated with "*to increase the strength*" or "*to get the strength back*".[231] We can read this verb in the *Pyramid Texts* (Chapter 1282, b) and also in the *Coffin Texts* (Chapter 1013). In both texts the dead, after drinking milk or beer (both considered revitalizing drinks), recovers his force and comes back to life: "*...I came back and I recovered the strength in nsrsr island" (ii.n.i swt.n.i nsrsr)*.[232] The use of the hair hieroglyph as determinative makes sense here; if the hair is an energy source and the aim of an Egyptian funeral is the resurrection of the corpse, it is to be expected to find it related to a verb meaning "*to fortify*". Furthermore, *swt* is a causative verb that derives from *wt*, with the translation "*to be powerful*" or "*to be big*".[233] In addition, wt also means "*to embalm*".[234] One of the main aims of embalming was to reconstruct the whole body - the physical reconstruction as the soul's support - and this consolidation seems to be connected to the hair element.

According to what we have seen here, there were two main aspects related to the lock of hair *swt* in Egyptian funerary belief. On one hand the *swty*, or the two locks of hair, could be considered an image of Isis and Nephthys, the two mourning goddesses who assisted the mummy in its resurrection. On the other hand, the word *swt* could have a

↑ Fig. 24
Mourners in the funerary cortège from the tomb of Ramose (TT55). Dynasty XVIII. Thebes. Photo: María Rosa Valdesogo.

double meaning as well: it could refer to the damage and the pain felt by the dead (so it would be directly related to the lament) and it could also refer to the power needed by the deceased for his rebirth.

5. Shaking and/or pulling hair in the direction of the mummy

Both the common mourners and the two mourners in the role of Isis and Nephthys

---

231 D. Meeks, 1977-1979, II, p.311, n° 78.3367; D. Meeks, 1976, p.88, n.14.

232  Translation of P. Barguet (P. Barguet, 1986, p.417).

233 *Wb* IV, 77, 9.

234 *Wb* I, 378, 8.

shook and pulled their hair in funerals, but did they make these gestures at the same time or with a similar meaning? In the Ancient Egyptian funerary ceremony, groups of mourning women can be seen as a part of the procession accompanying the rest of the people in the procession (priests, bearers, relatives, etc.) Those women are depicted weeping, moving, raising their arms, with their hands up (fig. 24) and also sometimes with dishevelled hair, shaking their hair or pulling locks of hair.

In these same scenes the corpse is transported by land and by water accompanied by two women standing at both ends of the coffin (fig. 25). These women are sometimes identified as Isis and Nephthys and sometimes as *ḏrt*. This Egyptian word meant "*kite*" and was used for naming the two women who played the role of Isis and Nephthys at

← Fig. 25
Wooden model of the funerary boat of Ukhhotep. The two mourners are standing at both ends of the bier. Meir? Dynasty XII. Metropolitan Museum of Art of New York, 12.183.3. Photo: Metropolitan Museum of Art of New York.

funerals. In the Osiris myth, Isis as a kite placed herself on top of the phallus of Osiris and could so conceive Horus, the avenger of his father's death and heir to the throne of Egypt. Therefore, Egyptian iconography, especially from the New Kingdom represented Isis and Nephthys as kites at both ends of the corpse.

5.1. Two mourners, two Kites. The two women in the role of Isis and Nephthys

According to funerary texts, in the mythical sphere Isis and Nephthys carried out a mourning rite by shaking and pulling their hair (*nwn / nwn m*). However, this is not shown in the funerary iconography of tombs. In the scenes of funerary processions, the two women in the role of the two goddesses appear in a complete hieratic attitude. They do not move and they do not gesticulate. The question is why? Were they different from the rest of the 'common' mourners? Had they, as representatives of Isis and Nephthys, a different role from just weeping over the dead?

At this point it is necessary to know more about the role of these two "different" mourners. If Isis and Nephthys in Egyptian mythology were the assistants of Osiris in his resurrection process, we have to look for information in documents related to the festival of Osiris. The best texts for this are *The Lamentations of Isis and Nephthys*[235] and *The Songs of Isis and Nephthys,*[236] both dating to the Ptolemaic Period. These two manuscripts consisted of lamentations read aloud by two women personifying Isis and Nephthys and were addressed to Osiris during the festivities at the Osiris temples.[237] Some important information can be obtained from both texts.

5.1.1. Remarks about the songs of Isis and Nephthys.

From this text we can deduct that one of the requirements these two women had to meet was to not having given birth and to not having become a mother yet.[238] Like the two goddesses in the myth, the two mourners in the role of Isis and Nephthys had to have the faculty of conceiving intact. We also have to consider that Horus was the first and only son of Isis, so if the mourner was the personification of that goddess, she could not have given birth yet[239].

To reinforce this concept, we can refer to the third tale of the "*Tales of King Cheops' Court*",[240] in which king Snefru wants to be sailed around the palace lake by twenty young women. When describing what the requirements of these women were, line 5,11 uses the sentence "*that they have not been opened with birth*" *(n wpt.sn m mst)*. Although it was often assumed that this meant "*virgin*", it seems evident that the literal meaning is "*that they have not yet become a mother* ". So maybe we should assume that one of the requirements for being a professional mourner in the role of Isis and Nephthys[241] was that the condition of that person would have had to be as similar as possible to Isis, who gave birth for the first (and only) time to her son Horus after the resurrection of Osiris.

Another requirement for these two women is that their body hair had to be removed:

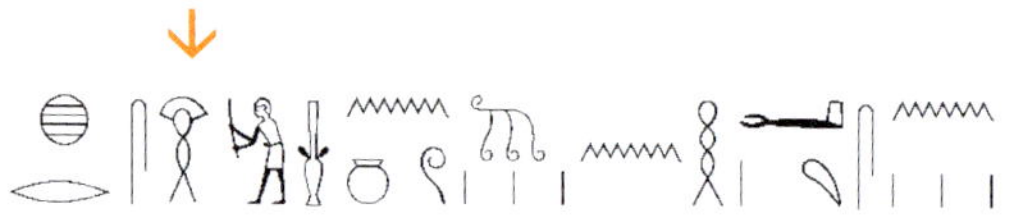

(*ḫsrw šnw n ḥꜥ.sn*). That seems to be directly related to the former requirement of "*pure of body*". In fact, that is a characteristic of liturgies in Ancient Egypt, where the entire

235 Pap. Berlín 3008. It is a hieratic text included in the *Book of the Dead* of a woman.

236 Pap. British Museum 10188. Also known as *The Bremner-Rhind Papyrus*.

237 Lichtheim, 1980, p.116.

238 *Vide supra* p 41.

239 Ph. Derchain also mentioned that two childless women were needed (Derchain, 1975, p.73). It is also interesting to note that in the myth of Osiris Isis has not yet given birth to Horus. He is born after his father's death and his birth is the guarantee of the resurrection of Osiris. In the funerary ceremony the idea would be the same: maternity takes place after death.

240 Papyrus Westcar.

241 A *ḏrt* or "kite".

priestly class had their body shaven for religious offices. So, in this case, the two mourners in the role of Isis and Nephthys officiating with no body hair makes sense.

So what about the head hair? Immediately after these lines, a confusing sentence follows, where we read: ↓

↑

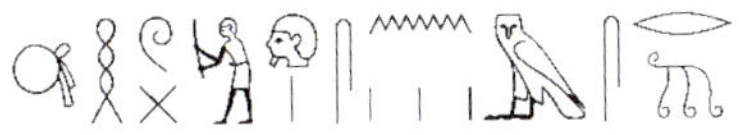

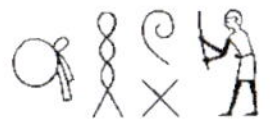

(*mḏḥ(w) tp.sn m sr*). The verb *mḏḥ* means "*to put something around the head*," usually a diadem. And the word *sr*, according to Ermand and Grapow, can refer to an artificial wig

↓

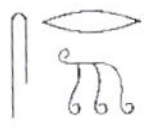

for a woman (in fact, Faulkner translated it as "*wig*") or to animal hair.[242] If we take this literally, what the text is saying is that the two women representing Isis and Nephthys should be wearing wigs. However, Hans Goedicke suggested that if *mḏḥ* meant "*to put around the head*", the word *sr* could be translated as "*hair band*".[243] A recent interpretation of Thomas Schneider suggests that the word sr could mean "*bristle*".[244]

Although the sentence is unclear, the text confirms that these two women had to have their body shaven, but not the head, where they had to have *sr*. That makes us think of the image of the two *ḏrt* in the funerary processions, where they can be seen with short hair and a band around the head or also with long hair but covered with a head-cloth (fig. 8). Did the word *sr* in *The Songs of Isis and Nephthys* refer to dishevelled hair, to short hair, to a wig, or to covered hair? The text also alludes to these two women as *ḥnskty,* "*the two with tresses*".[245] Again, this is a case of metonymy, where the two mourners Isis and Nephthys are identified by their most representative part, their hair.[246]

On the other hand, the manuscript contains some sentences in which the hieroglyph of hair appears isolated, apparently making no sense. However, when

reading the text more carefully, it seems that its presence in the papyrus was not a mistake of the scribe. In line 1,13 the two mourners are addressing Osiris saying (*ḥnty (?) m-ḫt tš.k r.n*). R.O. Faulkner considered

↓

242   *Wb* IV, p.191.

243   Goedicke, 1970, pp.244-266.

244   Schneider, 2007, p.312.

245   *ḏd mdw in ḥnskty* (*The Songs...* 1,9; 3,23; 6,23; 11,18)

246   *Vide supra* p.48.

PART II | **Shaking and Pulling hair**

that the hieroglyph in this sentence was an abbreviation of the Egyptian expression:

gm wš, which meant "*found defective*". So he concluded that the scribe had indicated a gap in the manuscript.[247] But, the hieroglyph is also an abbreviation of *šnỉ* and *smꜣ*,

both words meaning "*hair*". Taking this into consideration, the sentence could be transliterated in the following way: *ḫnty smꜣ/šnỉ m-ḫt tš.k r.n*, and translated as "(*Osiris you are*) *The one who is in front of the hair after you moved away from us*".[248] It would decribe the moment in which Osiris, the dead, is in front of the hair of Isis and Nephthys, the lament.

We find a very similar case in line 9,21: The transliteration of this sentence would be:

ỉꜣkb.sn n.k m ỉꜣr msb.(*w*) *smꜣw/šnw tp* or *bbw*(*t*) *tp.* R.O. Faulkner translated "*They mourn for you in dishevelment* (?), *the hair of their heads disordered* (?)." The word *ỉꜣr,*

which this scholar translated as "*dishevelment*", means "*sadness*" or "*lament*";[249] and the verb *ms/msb* refers to the gesture of "*to present*", "*to extend*", "*to bring*".[250] If we consider that the written word is *bbwt* (instead of *smꜣ* or *šnw*), we should translate it, according to certain scholars, as "*wig*".[251] So, the sentence could be translated in the following manner: "*They mourn for you with sadness, presenting the hair/wig of the head.*" Thinking about the gesture made by mourners during the funerary ceremony of shaking their hair forwards, it makes sense to assume that the text is referring exactly to that movement of throwing the mane of hair or addressing a lock of hair as a ritual gesture towards Osiris/ the dead.

Finally we have to mention line 11, 9: This is a very confusing sentence that R.O. Faulkner

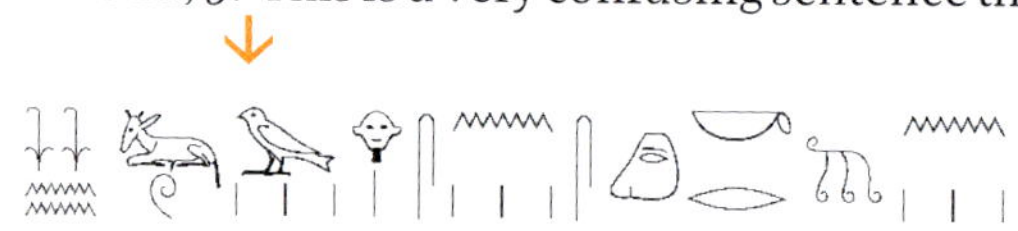

did not translate and which might mean something like: "*The discontent and the sorrow is over them (Isis and Nephthys?), can you be put in front of their hair*" (*nn ỉw ḥr.sn sḫnt.k r smꜣw.*(*s*)*n / šnw.*(*s*)*n*). In the previous sentences we read: "*They join your body for you*

247 Faulkner, 1936, p.132.

248 "*...after you moved away from us*" would be a way of saying "*...when you died*".

249 *Wb* I, 32, 2.

250 *Wb* II, 135.

251 *Wb* I, 455.

with the lament (or *while mourning), they go to take care of your corpse*".[252] In fact, from line 11,4 on, the action happens in the context of the moan made by the two representatives of Isis and Nephthys. It is important to demonstrate that mourning the dead god and assembling his body happens together; Isis and Nephthys take care of the mummy and they mourn the dead, and in this action their hair appears to be an important element, which the sacred text needs to mention.

In these three examples it seems that the text refers to the two women's hair when they assist the mummy of Osiris. It is the moment in which, according to the myth, they mourn the death of the god by shaking and/or pulling their hair, and they contribute to the restoration of the corpse. Both things together would help the final resurrection of Osiris. These mourning practices had a crucial role in funerals in Ancient Egypt. They were not just a sign of pain because of the beloved's death, but they were a group of gestures necessary for the dead's resurrection.

5.2. Context for the mourning gestures of shaking and/or pulling the hair at Ancient Egyptian funerals: how? why? when? where?

We have already seen that the *nwn* gesture of covering the face with the hair, *smꜣ*, made by the representatives of Isis and Nephthys was a way of returning to the primeval moment, to the primordial waters *(Nwn),* where the creation of a new human being (*nwnw, nnw, nn*) [253] was conceived. To pull a lock of hair would also be full of meaning, since the lock *swt* would symbolize the mourner it belongs to and would also be a gesture of sending a reviving force to the dead. Now the question remains if we can discern how this occurred exactly during an Egyptian funeral. Will we be able to answer how, when, why and where it happened?

5.2.1. How did Egyptian mourners shake and/or pull their hair in the funerary Ceremony?

According to iconography, common mourners made these gestures during the funerary procession. However, in the funerary retinue the two mourners representing Isis and Nephthys usually appear standing at both ends of the coffin in a static position. At first sight they do not seem to perform any special gesticulation next to the mummy, but the funerary texts describe that they did make special gestures with their hair in favour of the dead.

We have seen before how in Chapter 180 of the *Book of the Dead* the mourners were *"dishevelled for"* or *"over the deceased".*[254] In this chapter the dead needs to regain his phys-

252 *The Songs...*, 11, 7-8.

253 *nwnw, nww, nn* means "*young*", "*new*", "*healthy*" (*Wb* II, 215, 20), which would reinforce this idea of a revitalising act.

254 *Vide supra* p.20

ical powers, such as mobility, breathing, eyesight or virility, and in this process the two mourners are present, dishevelling their hair.[255] There are two exceptional iconographic documents linked to this text. One of them is the stele of Abkaou, chief of the cattle, in the Louvre Museum, which was found in Abydos and dates to Dynasty XI (fig. 4). In the Middle Kingdom it became very popular to erect a stele in Abydos in memory of the dead god Osiris. On this specific stele the lower register shows Abkaou and his wife receiving the offerings, while in an upper register there is an image of the ceremonies that took place during the Osiris festival. The celebration recalled the myth of Osiris, and a group of practices commemorated each episode: the death of Osiris, the mourning, the recovery of his body, his burial, his resurrection, etc. Among the many ceremonies, the stele shows a mourning scene, in which two unidentified women are bending over the horizontal corpse and both shake their mane of hair forwards in a perfect *nwn* gesture. We may assume that these two women were the two representatives of Isis and Nephthys, who re-enacted the mourning episode of the legend.

Along the same line we have to take into account a straightforward scene from Dynasty XVIII that belongs to the tomb of Renni in el-Kab. The mummy of Renni is lying on the funerary bed while a priest is officiating (maybe making a libation) next to the corpse's head; meanwhile a woman at the feet of the corpse appears shaking her hair towards the body. According to the inscription, she is "*his sister*", an identification that could be full of meaning. The myth of Osiris belongs in the mythical context we are discussing; the dead person (in this case Renni) is in the Egyptian view identified with the god, and Isis is Osiris's sister. This kinship between Osiris and Isis is mentioned in many documents, for instance, in the *Songs of Isis and Nephthys* we read "*Can you copulate with your sister Isis*"[256] or in Papyrus Louvre about the ceremony of the glorification of Osiris, the goddess addresses Osiris, saying: "*I am your sister Isis*"[257] and we have seen that in the tomb of Petosiris it is written how "*Isis joined the limbs of her brother*" Osiris.[258] So, the main mourner, who should play the role of Isis, was the "*sister of the dead*".

The mortuary temple of Seti I in Dra Abu el-Naga contains also a very clear funerary scene. The mummy is lying on the bier and he is assisted by two women at both ends of him. These two women appear shaking their mane of hair towards the body. These three examples reflect what is said in Chapter 180 of *Book of the Dead* and make us think that at some point during the funerary ceremony the mourners in the role of Isis and Nephthys made the *nwn* gesture of shaking their hair forwards, pointing the mane directly to the mummy.

What about the gesture of pulling the lock of hair (*nwn m swt*)? According to the documents this is a gesture that not only the common mourners made, but also Isis and Nephthys. Funerary texts show clearly the relationship between these two goddesses

---

255 Chapter 180 of the *Book of the Dead* was also included in many royal tombs of the New Kingdom (Tutmosis III, Seti I, Ramses II, Meneptah I, Seti II, Siptah, Ramses III and Ramses IV) and in every case the verb used for "*disheveled*" was *nwn*, which clearly refers to the gesture of shaking the hair forwards.

256 *Songs*...5, 25.

257 Roeder, 1960, p.182.

258 Daumas, 1960, p.68, pl.I.

and the lock of hair *swt*, and the iconography from the New Kingdom onwards also includes images of Isis and Nephthys pulling their lock of hair in its funerary repertoire. The head end of the coffin of Ramses IV has two images of Isis and Nephthys, on the left and on the right side, pulling their lock of hair (the *nwn m swt* gesture).[259] Their position on the sarcophagus seems to indicate that they were making this gesture oriented directly towards the mummy of the pharaoh. At both sides an inscription accompanies the image, the left inscription reads: *"They move their faces during the moan; they mourn over the secret corpse of š who is in front of Duat. Both goddesses are holding their locks of hair swt....*" In the tomb of Ramses IX there is a scene from the *Book of the Caverns* depicted on the left wall of the burial chamber.[260] It is integrated in a sequence of episodes representing the resurrection of the deceased. The dead appears as a mummy inside an oval, four women are bent over the corpse and are making the *nwn m swt* gesture of pulling their locks of hair directly towards the body (fig. 23). In the following scene the dead is not a mummy anymore; now his legs and arms move, i.e. show signs of new life, as if it was a result of the previous action. That makes us think about the *nwn m* gesture as something made in order to revitalize the body. The text accompanying the image is a fragment of the *Book of Caverns* in which we read about the resurrection of the dead: *"Those Goddesses are so, they are mourning over the secret place of Osiris...they are together, screaming and crying over the secret place of the ceremony... their secret is in their fingers...."*[261]

The text does not mention Isis and Nephthys, but rather "*those Goddesses*" who mourn; on the other hand, there are not two of them, but four. At this point it is important to understand that in Egyptian belief Isis, Nephthys, Neith and Serket formed a team of four for the protection of the dead. The inscription does not clarify the identity of these four goddesses, but the important point here is that they are mourning women, who pull their lock of hair towards the dead, and afterwards the mummy is revitalized. So, the connection between mourning and the resurrection of the dead, towards whom the women are pulling their locks of hair, is clear. It is also interesting to focus on the expression *"...their secret is in their fingers..."*, because with those fingers they are holding their hair. What is meant in this formulation as the secret? Perhaps the lock of hair? We will return to that point later.

The image of Isis and Nephthys making the *nwn m swt* gesture becomes popular on many *sarcophagi* from later periods of Egyptian history. For instance, the coffin of the dwarf Dyedhor,[262] who was a dancer at the Serapeum, was found at Saqqara, dating to the Persian Period. It shows Isis and Nephthys pulling their locks of hair. Or the sarcophagus of the royal scribe Nes-shu-tefnut[263] from the Ptolemaic Period also found at Saqqara. This sarcophagus also includes the scene of these two goddesses pulling their lock of hair. The inscribed text refers to this gesture, saying: "*...the two goddesses who pull their hair. There is water coming forth from the jars, which stems from the eyes of the*

259 *Vide supra* p.46.

260 *Vide supra* p.46.

261 Author's translation.

262 Louvre Museum, D9.

263 Kunsthistorisches Museum in Vienna, 1.

two goddesses,[264] like blood; the inhabitants of the Netherworld breathe on account of it...."

All these examples lead us to interpret that in the Egyptian belief, at least from the New Kingdom onwards, in some moment prior to the resurrection, the dead counted on the help of Isis and Nephthys who lean their faces forward, holding their locks of hair, *swt*, and cry over the corpse, allowing the dead to breathe and to be revived.

Summed up, Ancient Egyptian mourners in the role of Isis and Nephthys performed a rite during the funeral with their hair. In these gestures their face could be covered with the hair (*nwn*) or the lock of hair (*nwn m*) could be pulled. Both practices were executed in front of or over the corpse and always with the aim of revitalization.

5.2.2. Why did Egyptian mourners shake and/or pull their hair during the mourning rite?

The relationship between these mourning practices performed by the two professional mourners and the myth of Osiris now seems evident. According to the myth, Isis started crying and mourning the disappearance of her husband together with her sister Nephthys. Once the many parts of Osiris's body were collected, they were joined together with the help of Anubis. However, although the body of Osiris was reunited, he needed to recover some vital powers for his new life, that is, he needed to complete his resurrection. At that moment the magic power of Isis, assisted by Nephthys, came into play. Isis, and Nephthys by extension, became kites flapping their wings over the corpse of Osiris, blowing air into his nose. This way, Isis and Nephthys gave him back his breath. When Osiris could breathe again, he started recovering some other powers and he began to awake.

But the resurrection was still not completed. The myth informs us that, while Osiris was dead and his resurrection was still in process, Seth proclaimed himself ruler of Egypt. The country was now ruled by a usurper, a problem that Isis had to solve. The goddess not only had to bring Osiris back to life, she also had to conceive a son from Osiris to produce a rightful heir to the throne. This son would avenge the murder, would eliminate Seth and would become the legitimate king of Egypt. Therefore, apart from the breath, Osiris needed to recover his virility as well. Once again, with the myth is explained how Isis, as a kite, placed herself on top of the phallus of her dead husband, aroused him and consummated the union. This way she conceived Horus, the posthumous son of Osiris, the legitimate heir and the future king of Egypt.

These two aspects (breath and virility) of the myth of Osiris were crucial to the final resurrection and Isis as a kite was primarily responsible for this, with Nephthys as her assistant. So, on earth, this part of the myth had to be reproduced and became a part of the funerary rite to assure the dead's resurrection. At this point it seems logical to assume that Egyptian priests made an adaptation for the funerary ceremony. The two kites

264 In front of Isis and Nephthys there are four gods pouring water from jars. According to the text this symbolises the tears of the two mourning goddesses.

in the myth who flap their wings over the corpse of Osiris became the two professional mourning women in the rite, who, as representatives of Isis and Nephthys, shook and/or pulled their hair over the mummy.

5.2.3. In which Moment of the Funeral Did Egyptian Mourners Perform their Mourning Gestures Related to Hair?

During Egyptian burials, two professional mourning women thus played the role of Isis and Nephthys and they performed a mourning rite shaking and/or pulling their hair over the corpse. With this practice they re-enacted the part of the legend of Osiris in which Isis as a kite gave back breath and virility to Osiris. Groups of common mourners were also part of the funerary ensemble, and among them some women were shaking or pulling their hair. Now the question is: can we deduce when in the funerary ritual this took place? That is, were the mourning rites of the professional mourners and the mourning gestures of the common mourners performed throughout the entire funeral? Or had each mourner her own moment for performing that gesture? And if that was the case, at which moment of the funerary ceremony did the mourning rites and the mourning gestures with the hair take place exactly?

← Fig. 26
Scene of funerary cortège in a rishi coffin. Thebes. Dynasty XVII. Photo: Metropolitan Museum of Art of New York.

Here, Egyptian iconography is very helpful, because it shows some differences between the common mourners and the two women in the role of Isis and Nephthys. Usually the common mourners appear in a dynamic way; the artist tried to express the movement of their gestures when they accompany the coffin during the procession, as can be seen in the mastabas of Mereruka (fig.5) and Idu (fig. 6); on a Middle Kingdom coffin from Abydos, where the mourner bending her body and shaking her hair, walks next to the dead[265]; or on a *rishi* coffin from Dynasty XVII from el-Assassif (Thebes),[266] where a group of seven mourners accompanies the bier while making gestures of pain (fig. 26). In these cases, the women shaking or pulling their hair are all bending over, walking or moving in some way. But elsewhere the common mourners appear to be static; that is, they cry while sitting or standing in a calm manner and sometimes they even make the *nwn* gesture. We can see this for instance in the tombs of Rekhmire (fig. 2), Amenemhat or Inneni or on Ostracon 5886 from the Manchester Museum (fig. 33). In these scenes the groups of mourning women seem to be near the tomb. From the iconography we can

265 Fitzwilliam Museum E.283a.1900.

266 Metropolitan Museum of Art of New York, 14.10.1a, b.

deduce that the mourning gestures of shaking and pulling the hair made by common mourners took place at two different moments during the funeral: firstly during the procession, while the coffin was transported and while they were accompanying the corpse, and secondly after the arrival at in the necropolis, when the retinue was close to the burial place, at the door of the tomb, and apparently while the body was being buried.

Regarding the two professional mourners, the situation seems to be different. Documents demonstrate that they also made those gestures of shaking and/or pulling their hair, not so much during the procession but in the presence of the mummy. The two mourners representing Isis and Nephthys would be two women selected to represent a divine role. Maybe their mourning ritual with the hair was part of a group of practices executed for the resurrection of the dead. At Ancient Egyptian funerals, the main ceremony for restoring the powers of the deceased was the Opening of the Mouth (fig. 27). It was a group of practices based on the myth of Osiris and was made over the mummy or over the statue of the dead for granting him final resurrection. The Opening of the Mouth rites were mainly performed by the *sem* priest, the lector priest and the two mourners identified as "kites".[267]

→ Fig. 27
Part of the Opening of the Mouth ceremony from the tomb of Rekhmire (TT100). Thebes. Dynasty XVIII. Photo: María Rosa Valdesogo.

Originally, the Opening of the Mouth Ceremony was possibly executed consecutively

267 The most complete representation of the Opening of the Mouth Ceremony is in the tomb of Rekhmire in Thebes from the XVIII Dynasty (TT 100). According to this scene, the "resurrection team" performing this ceremony consisted of many people. Apart from the lector priest, the *sem* priest and the two kites, there were: the rpat (representing the firstborn son), the *sꜣ-mr.f* ("*beloved son*"), the *smr* ("*friend*"), the *imy-is* ("*the one who is inside the tomb*" and who would represent Anubis), the *imy-ḫnt* ("*the one in the antechamber*") and the *msntiw* ("*the workers*"). This ceremony also appears in a less complete version in the tomb of Menna (TT 69), Djehoutymes (TT 295) and Renni in el-Kab (EK 7), all from Dynasty XVIII. The first royal tomb which includes the Opening of the Mouth Ceremony is the tomb of Tutankhamon (KV 62); and in the XIX Dynasty it becomes more common, the most complete version being in the tomb of Seti I (KV 17) and the tomb of Tauseret and Setnakht (KV 14).

with the mummification process. In fact, if the goal was the resurrection of the dead following the myth of Osiris, it makes sense to assume that the revitalizing practices took place just after the restoration of the body. Exactly as it happened in the myth: Anubis restored the body of Osiris and afterwards Isis and Nephthys with their magical power executed a mourning rite and brought Osiris back to life. The aim of the Opening of the Mouth Ceremony was to restore all the powers the deceased needed for his resurrection and his new life in the Hereafter: breathing, eyesight, mobility and sexuality.... It seems probable that the mourners in the role of Isis and Nephthys performed the mourning rite with their hair near the mummy, at some moment during the Opening of the Mouth Ceremony. In fact, Egyptian iconography offers some good indications that this was indeed the case. The most evident is the scene in the tomb of Renni in el-Kab: we can see how the priest is doing the resurrection ritual over the corpse and the statue of the dead, while a mourner is making the *nwn* gesture next to him (fig. 28).

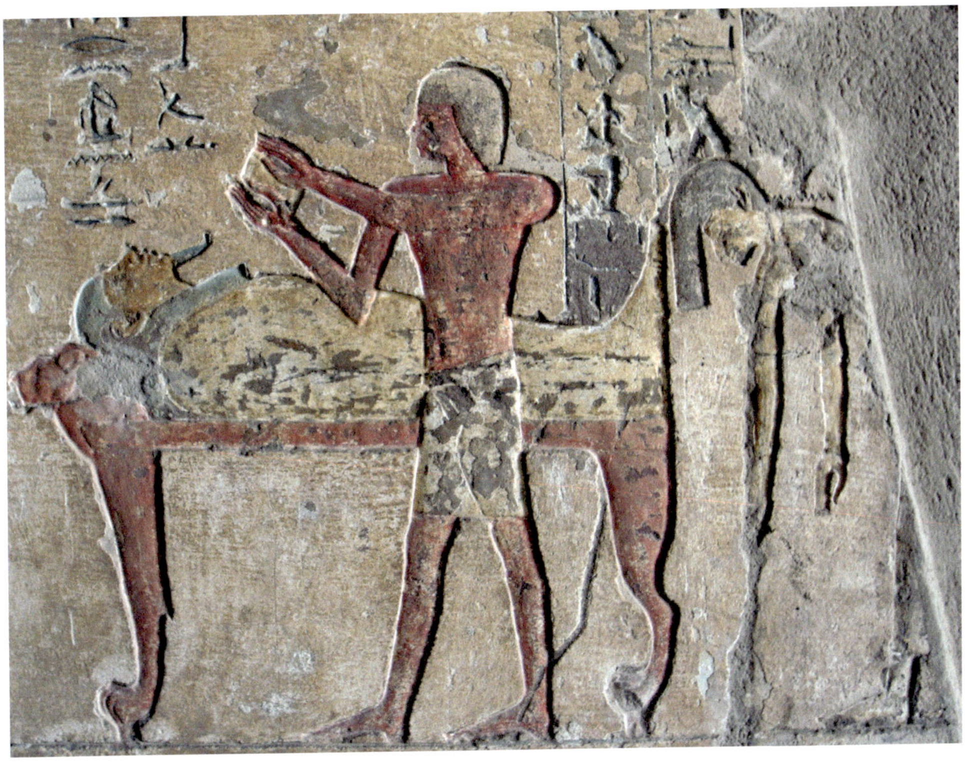

← **Fig. 28**
Detail of the Opening of the Mouth ceremony from the tomb of Renni (EK7). El-Kab. Dynasty XVIII. Photo: © www.osirisnet.net

5.2.3.1. A Remark about the stele of Abkaou

At this point I would like to mention again the stele of Abkaou[268] from Dynasty XI (fig. 4). Two mourning women are shaking their hair over the mummy with three hieroglyphs between them: the sledge, which is the phoneme *tm,* and two adzes or hoes

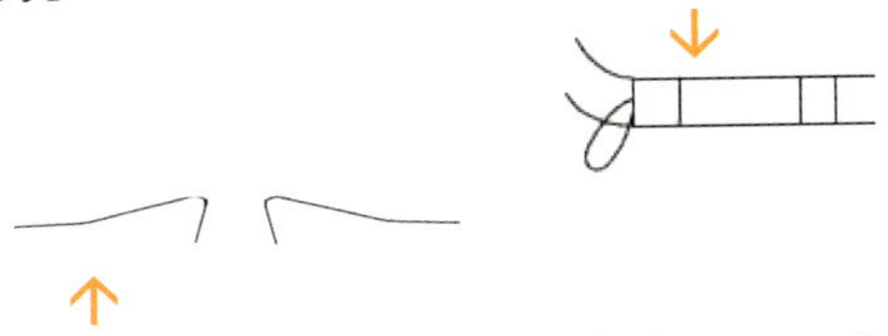

nwty. What does this inscription mean?

268 The Louvre Museum, C15.

The verb *tm* in Ancient Egyptian means "*to complete*", "*to be completed*", "*to join the different parts of the body*",[269] especially in the sense of joining the limbs of the dead.[270] The two hoes could be related to the verb *nwi*, which means "*to be in charge of*".[271] So, the inscription could be translated as "*to be in charge of completing*". In the Myth of Osiris, Isis and Nephthys are the ones who collect the different parts of the body of Osiris, which were afterwards assembled by Anubis, so these two mourners in the image would also be in charge of mending the body of the dead.

There is also another possible interpretation. The two hoes *nwty* are mentioned in Chapter 258 of the *Pyramid Texts*, where the dead king is identified with Osiris. This chapter treats the restoration of the deceased, and in it we read "*...his injuries are effaced by the two kites of Osiris...his sister, the Lady of Pe,*[272] *is the one who cries for him...Unas...he satisfies the two hoes in Hermopolis...*".[273] So, three important aspects are connected here: the lament, the restoration of the body and the two adzes. All three are on the stele of Abkaou. And later on in Egyptian iconography the hoe will be the main indicator referring to the Opening of the Mouth Ceremony. So, the *nwn* gesture the two mourners of this stele are making over the body could be part of the practises of revitalizing the deceased. The relationship between the two mourning women and their mourning rite with the hair and the restoration of the mummy seems quite clear. In Egyptian funerary practices the restoration of the mummy was achieved through the Opening of the Mouth Ceremony. It seems logical that those gestures of shaking and/or pulling hair towards the dead were performed by the two professional mourners representing Isis and Nephthys as part of the Opening of the Mouth Ceremony.

5.2.4. The professional mourning rite as a part of thc opening of the mouth ceremony

Now the question remains at which moment during the Opening of the Mouth Ceremony the mourning rite was performed. Although much has been written about this ceremony, little is known about all the practices which were part of it, or if those practices had to follow a predetermined order. Taking into consideration that the most complete scene of this rite is the one depicted inside the tomb of Rekhmire (fig. 29), I would like to consider that the practics that were depicted there and their order, represent what really happened during this ceremony. It is probably true that there may have also been more simple versions of the Opening of the Mouth Ceremony. For these ceremonies, I would also take as a basis the depiction from the tomb of Rekhmire. So, in general outline (later we will discuss this in more detail) the sequence would be: to prepare the mummy (or the statue), to perform the rite of *tekenu*, to make gestures for opening the mouth of the mummy, to perform the mourning rite and to make final offers to the resurrected dead.

269 *Wb* V, 303.

270 *Wb* V, 305, 1.

271 *Wb* II, 220.

272 Isis and Nephthys were the "*Ladies of Pe and Dep*", the two localities which later become Buto.

273 *Pyr.*, 311.

There are even different theories regarding the place where the ceremony was performed and how many people were involved. Let us imagine that after the embalming of the corpse, the procession proceeded to the necropolis. Having arrived there, presumably inside the tomb, the Opening of the Mouth Ceremony for transmitting the vital powers back to the mummy took place, and the two representatives of Isis and Nephthys took part in it. But do we know what really happened inside the tomb? How every rite was performed? Many sources mention the Opening of the Mouth Ceremony, but usually these sources are far from explicit. The ceremony is predominantly depicted in reliefs and paintings from the New Kingdom in an abbreviated way, with the lector priest and/or the *sem* priest is holding the utensils used in the ritual (mainly the adze and the stone vessels) performed on the mummy. Meanwhile, the two mourners (or sometimes just one) are crying close to the dead. In some cases, the scene has a more divine nuance and the one officiating is Anubis, while Isis and Nephthys stand at both ends of the corpse.[274] From New Kingdom sources, we know that the Opening of the Mouth was a complex ceremony, at least during that period of Egyptian history. It did not just consist of touching the mummy's mouth with the adze and reciting some sacred texts; numerous practices were part of it, many tools were needed and more people than just one person were involved; according to the documents, at least the lector priest, the *sem* priest and the two professional mourners in the role of Isis and Nephthys took part in it.

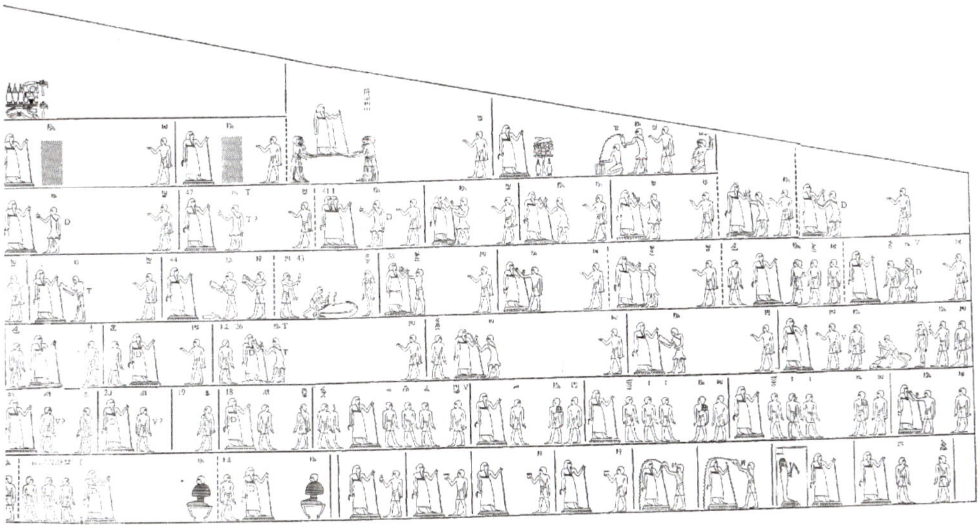

← Fig. 29
Opening of the Mouth ceremony from the tomb of Rekhmire (TT100). Thebes. Dynasty XVIII (After Otto, E., "Das ägyptische Mundöffnungsritual", ÄA 3, Wiesbaden, 1960.)

274 The presence of Anubis would fit in perfectly with the idea of the mummification and the resurrection ceremony happening together or consecutively in former times.

The most detailed documentation of the Opening of the Mouth Ceremony can be found on the south wall of the tomb of Rekhmire in Gourna (fig. 29). The rite is depicted step by step in a composition of fifty-three scenes. The broad outline which Rekhmire offers, is:

1. The statue of the deceased is put on a mound symbolizing the primordial hill.
2. The statue is purified with water, natron and incense.
3. The *sem* priest transmits the vital energy commemorating the Ancient Egyptian tradition of the sacrifice and rebirth of the *tekenu.*[275] The *sem* priest imitated the ancient victim curled up and wrapped in a cloth. The *sem* priest then rose from the cloth and held a brief dialogue with the lector priest:

Sem priest: *"I saved the eye from his mouth, I healed his leg"*

Lector priest: *"I have placed your eye, through which you revive."*[276]

4. The *sem* priest makes the first gestures of Opening the Mouth on the statue with the little finger.
5. The *mesentiu* (labourers) work on the statue (polishing and carving) as a creational gesture.[277]
6. Then the ox of Upper Egypt is sacrificed to restore the vitality of the deceased. The *sem* priest offers the animal's heart and foreleg to the statue. The big *ḏrt* as the representative of Isis is present here. The inscription shows a brief dialogue among the three:

Sem priest: *"to stretch the arms towards the bull ng of Upper Egypt"*

Slaughterer: *"get up over him, cut its foreleg and remove its heart"*

Thc big *ḏrt* says at his ear: *"Your lips have done that against you. Will your mouth open?"*

This part of the ceremony is very important to us, not just because of the presence of one of the professional mourners, but also because it seems to recall the conflict between Horus and Seth. According to J. C. Goyon this sequence took place when these two gods fought and Isis became a kite, landed on a tree and cried to Seth, who denounced his crime unconsciously: *"Cry over you. Your own mouth has said it. Your ability has judged you. What else?*[278]

7. After the sacrifice of the ox of Upper Egypt, the *sem* priest makes more gestures simulating the Opening of the Mouth towards the statue with magical tools:

---

275 We will not discuss the figure of the *tekenu* in detail here. It seems to be a human victim, whose origin dates to ancient times. The idea is that the death of a human being could be part of the early *heb Sed* to transmit vital energy to the pharaoh, helping him to renew his kingship.

276 E. Otto, 1960, p.71.

277 The sculptor was called *sʿnkh* in the ancient Egyptian language, which meant "*to make live*". This step would be taken when the ceremony was performed on a statue.

278 J.C.Goyon, 1972, p.121.

the *nṯrt ꜥdze* and the *wr-ḥkꜣw*; and with the ox's foreleg.

8. The statue is given to the *r-pꜥt*, the person who represented the heir,[279] and the *mesentiu* work again on the dead's image.

9. New opening gestures on the mouth of the deceased are made. After that, there is an offering of *ꜣbt* stones.[280]

10. The sacrifice of the ox of Lower Egypt. In this case the small *ḏrt*, the mourner representing Nephthys is present. And again, the animal's foreleg and heart are offered to the dead.

11. After the sacrifice of that ox, the priest again ritually opens the mouth of the deceased.

12. Finally, the funerary offerings are given to the statue and the *sem* priest pays his respects to the new soul who lives in the Hereafter. The final resurrection of Rekhmire is a fact.

The wall decorations demonstrate that the two professional mourners personifying Isis and Nephthys took part in the Opening of the Mouth Ceremony in the moment of killing the ox as a Sethian victim. Some other records (private and royal) also show the presence of these two women at that moment. The tomb of Wensu in Dra Abu el-Naga (TTA4)[281] shows a scene of the slaughter of the ox in the Opening of the Mouth Ceremony; the *sem* priest supervises the rite while the slaughterer is cutting the foreleg, and the two *ḏrty* stand in front of them. Also, the tomb of Amenemhat in Gourna (TT53) has among its decorative scenes the slaughtering of the ox in the presence of the professional mourner.[282] The tombs of Seti I (KV17) and of Tauseret and Setnakht (KV14) also contain some scenes of the Opening of the Mouth Ceremony with depictions of the slaughter of the ox which in both cases is made in front of the professional mourner. We further need to look at the tomb of Qar (fig. 31). Here, the Opening of the Mouth is apparently performed by the embalmer, the lector priest and one professional mourner, and the slaughtering of an ox is also depicted.[283]

Sources seem to show that the two professional mourners personifying Isis and Nephthys had an important role in the ritual for the resurrection of the deceased. They were members of the group of people who took care of the rebirth of the corpse in the Opening of the Mouth Ceremony and who re-enacted the myth of Osiris. Because of their presence during the slaughter of the ox we can consider that their mourning rite of shaking and/or pulling their hair towards the dead coincided with the moment of killing the Sethian victim. In my research I have tried to reconstruct the order in which these rituals happened.

---

279 *R-pꜥt* is a noun derived from the adjective *iry-pꜥt*, which means "the one being noble". *R-pꜥt* was literally "*prince*" (*Wb* II, 415, 15) or "*noble*" (Faulkner, p. 148). In the Opening of the Mouth Ceremony this priest played the role of the heir. In fact, the title *r-pꜥt nswt nṯrw* was a title of Horus, as rightful heir.

280 Some scholars consider the *ꜣbt* stones to symbolise the milk teeth. That would link to the concept of the deceased as a child.

281 A scribe of the accounts of grain from Dynasty XVIII. The tomb is now destroyed and what remains of it is thanks to former records dating from the XIXth century.

282 Otto, 1960, Abb. 2C.

283 *Vide infra* p.71.

If the mourning rite they performed was a ritual way of recalling the myth of Osiris, we might assume that the order of the acts was the same as in the myth itself. So the mourners would first shake and/or pull their hair towards the corpse, in this way they would revive the body by giving back the vital faculties, one of them being the virility to assure the birth of Horus. He was the one who would avenge the death of his father and he would kill Seth. So, in the rite the sacrifice of the ox, as the Sethian victim, would presumably happen after the sacred mourning gesture with the hair.

5.2.5. Where did the professional mourning rite happen during the Egyptian funeral?

In contrast to the common mourners, who are represented crying and weeping with arms raised, bending, kneeling, etc., the two women in the role of Isis and Nephthys, identified as *ḏrty*, usually stand in a very static manner at both ends of the coffin during the funerary procession. They stand and look at the mummy, but they never shed any tears, pull clothes, or move at all. However, we have seen that they carried out a mourning rite with their hair for the benefit of the dead. If we cannot see them perform this rite, was this mourning rite made by these two mourners, perhaps not a public practice? Maybe it was not visible to the members of the procession. Could it be a more private or secluded moment?

5.2.5.1 The professional mourning rite as a secret ritual

The mourning rite made by the *ḏrty* was part of the practices that, together, formed the Opening of the Mouth Ceremony for the mummy's rebirth (fig. 30). However, I have found that all the information from records (iconography, texts and epigraphy) is neither detailed nor clear. For instance, the stele of Abkaou from Abydos - especially due to its lack of inscription - needs a detailed explanation in order to understand the image of the hieroglyphs of the two adzes and the sledge between the two women shaking their hair.[284] The artist depicted the revitalizing Osirian rites, but the scenes are not explicit at all. The funerary ceremony in the mastaba of Qar is not detailed either. The practices of the resurrection of the dead are not represented at all, they are just hinted at.[285] Later in Egyptian history, the corpus of images in the tombs became larger and new funerary scenes appeared, which - together with the religious literature - give us a wider view on funerals in Ancient Egypt. From Dynasty XVIII onwards, the artisans were able to include more detailed scenes of the Opening of the Mouth Ceremony in the decorative program of some tombs. But even so, the ceremony was not depicted in an exhaustive manner and in some cases we have to deduce what really happened (as is the case with the episode of the slaughter of the ox in the presence of the professional mourner).

Why is the given information on the resurrection practices always so unclear? Perhaps on the stele of Abkaou the sculptor depicted the Opening of the Mouth Ceremony in

---

284 *Vide supra* p.60.

285 *Vide infra* p.70.

an abbreviated way; he included all the elements that appear later in the ceremony (mourners, priests, corpse, ritual tools), but in an abbreviated form. Even the scenes of the Opening of the Mouth Ceremony dating from the New Kingdom are not depicted in detail. With the exception of some tombs in which many steps of the entire ceremony are depicted, the ceremony is mainly represented by one image depicting a mummy or a coffin standing up and the funerary priest putting the adze to the dead's mouth (fig. 30). This leaves us with the impression that there was no intention of including the entire ceremony in the decorative program of the tombs. Was it common knowledge that there was a rite for reviving the dead? Did the artisan know how to depict it? Did he ignore the information he had to design? Or did he ignore what happened during that rite? Was it not a commonly known ceremony? All these questions raise with us the one question of whether this abbreviated way of depicting the Opening of the Mouth Ceremony was not a short version, but rather a codified way of representing a hidden ritual in the attempt of protecting the information of a secret rite.

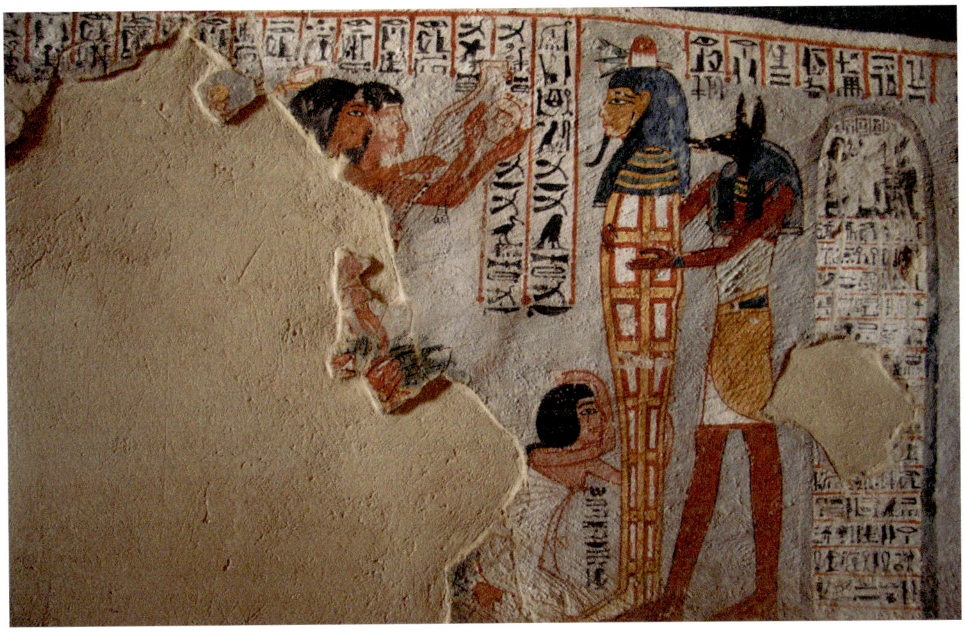

← Fig. 30
Opening of the Mouth ceremony from the tomb of Roy (TT255). Thebes. Dynasty XIX. Photo: Mª Rosa Valdesogo.

According to J. C. Goyon, in earlier times of Egyptian history, the Opening of the Mouth Ceremony was done inside the *ḥt-nbw* (*the Golden House*) as a sacred building, later the ceremony would be realized inside the tomb although always in a hidden manner.[286] Based on some scenes from tombs and papyri from the New Kingdom, in which the mummy is standing and priests and mourners are assisting the corpse as well. J. C. Goyon also suggests that the Opening of the Mouth Ceremony could be performed at the entrance of the tomb, but if that ceremony is meant to be kept out of sight, it does not seem possible to perform it in an open space.

The rejuvenating rites for the mummy's rebirth may have been a secret. And many funerary texts allude to this concept of covertness surrounding Osiris' death and resurrection. There are many sources, which refer to the moment of the resurrection process as a "secret matter". On the coffin of Ramses IV for instance we read how these mourning

286 Goyon, 1972, pp.95-96.

women were crying over the "*secret copse of the dead*".[287] In the resurrection scene in the tomb of Ramses IX with the four mourning women pulling their hair over the mummy (fig. 23), the texts refer to their mourning "*over the secret place of Osiris*", "*over the secret place of the ceremony*" and with "*their secret in their fingers*".[288] In the tomb of Ramses VI there is a scene from to the *Book of the Caverns* in which Isis and Nephthys appear raising the body of Osiris and the inscription on it reads that "*Osiris is in front of his secret*". Or, in Chapter 17 of the *Book of the Dead*, which deals with the moment of copulation between Isis and Osiris, the text clearly states that "*Isis has been on her secret*".[289]

It seems that in Ancient Egyptian belief, the mystery of death and resurrection was not accessible to all people. That would also explain why the *Book of the Dead* reads regarding Osiris's resurrection. "*...it is a secret of the Duat and a religious mystery in the deceased's kingdom... it is a mystery that cannot be known, to take care of the blessed heart give him movement, take away the bandage from his eyes, open his face.... Read that with no one seeing it, apart from your true friend and the lector priest.*"[290] Death itself was, for the dead person, an initiation to the Hereafter's mysteries.[291] Only the priests knew the secret of Osiris's death and resurrection, and keeping this secret was crucial to universal harmony.[292] Possibly for that reason the "night of Isis" hid the mysteries of resurrection.[293] Even Isis sometimes received the name "The Mysterious One", since she "*has been everything she has been, everything she is and everything she will be, and her veil, no mortal has ever taken off*".[294]

The Theban *Book of Breathing,* dating to the Ptolemaic Period, was a funerary text that was recited just before closing the lid of the coffin[295] and with it a mourning woman in the role of Isis gave a speech for reviving Osiris and for helping his soul ascend to the sky as the lunar disc: "*That is something that needs to be hidden. Do not let anyone read it. It is useful for one in the necropolis. He will live again successfully millions of times.*"[296] The Magical Papyrus Salt 825 (probably also from Ptolemaic Period) contains a text about the rite of the conservation of life. According to Ph. Derchain it was a group of ceremonies that was conducted annually and was directed to the mummy of Osiris, similar to the ceremonies of the month of Khoiak in Dendera[297], and they were "*to be read by a scribe of*

---

287 *Vide supra* p.56.

288 *Vide supra* p.56.

289 *Vide supra* p.45.

290 *LdM,* 148.

291 S. Mayassis, 1957, p.218.

292 S. Mayassis, 1957, p.42.

293 Sinesio, *Epist.*, XIII, v.s. 89; S. Mayassis, 1957, p.65.

294 Plutarco, *De Iside et Osiride*, 9.

295 J.Cl. Goyon, 1972, p.217.

296 *Book of the Breathing*, cf. Desroches-Noblecourt, 1968.

297 Ph. Derchain, 1964, p.75.

the workshop whose name is in the House of Life"[298]. It informs the reader that the "House of Life" is hidden, unknown and invisible. It is a "*secret book... contains life and death. Do not reveal it, the one who reveals it will die suddenly or be murdered*".[299] This leads to the idea that in Ancient Egypt the resurrection process was something that only concerned the deceased and the team helping him in his recovery, and it was not accessible to everybody.

Maybe the Egyptian artists of the New Kingdom, with those abbreviated scenes of the Opening of the Mouth in front of the tomb were just indicating what happened inside the tomb; the image was only an allusion to what happened inside. The actual process would be that, after the mummification, the procession walked to the necropolis. Once there, the Opening of the Mouth Ceremony, and the mourning rite with the gestures made with the hair, took place inside the tomb. While the rest of the procession would wait outside the tomb, the professional mourning rite, as a part of the Opening of the Mouth Ceremony, would be performed in there. Inside the tomb the two women in the role of Isis and Nephthys shook their hair forwards (*nwn* gesture) and/or pulled their frontal lock of hair (*nwn m* gesture) towards the corpse to help in the dead's resurrection.

5.2.5.2. Some remarks on the funerary ceremony in the tomb of Qar

From an iconographical point of view there are many examples that direct our thoughts to a similar conclusion. In the tomb of Qar at Giza, dating to Dynasty VI, the funerary procession is represented on the north wall of Court C with all the personnel taking part in the ceremony (fig. 31): the two professional mourners (the two kites *ḏrty*) with short hair accompanying the coffin, the *wt* priest (the embalmer), the *ẖr-ḥb* (lector priest) and the rest of the funerary staff. According to Simpson, the normal order of the funerary scenes on the wall was, from the top downwards; so from left to right in the upper register and from right to left in the lower one. Therefore, the sequence would start with

↓ Fig. 31
Funerary procession from the tomb of Qar. Giza. Dynasty VI (After Simpson, W. K., *The Mastabas of Qar and Idu*. G7101 and 7102. Boston, 1976, fig. 24.)

298 Gardiner, 1938, p. 167. The "House of Life" was the Egyptian institution linked to kingship and temples, where knowledge was created and preserved. It was a library, a scientific center, a school, and an archive, where manuscripts were written...The House of Life in Papyrus Salt 825 is depicted like a building in Abydos of four bodies; inside the building was Osiris and at each corner were Thoth, Horus, Isis and Nephthys; the ceiling was Nut and the floor was Geb.

299 Ph. Derchain, 1964, p.139.

the two mourners and the embalmer and would end with the arrival at the building on the left, which was considered to be the embalming place.[300] However, it does not seem logical that the final image of the complete scene is at the bottom of the wall, when the image of the resurrected Qar in front of his food offerings is at the top. If we maintain Simpson's theory, it is really difficult to understand the logical sequence of the different moments in the Qar's funerary ceremony.

A clue to another interpretation and order in which we are supposed to view these scenes in their true order or sequence, is in a small scene at the right end of the second register, where one of the mourners appears facing the embalmer. Both are uttering some words and behind the embalmer the lector priest is situated. Between them, above the altar with food offerings, an inscription says: "*ḏꜣt rꜣ*". Looking at the gestures (hand on mouth) we could suppose that the short sentence is only literally describing the position of the hand on the mouth. However, the expression "*ḏꜣt rꜣ*" was also used in Ancient Egypt as referring to "*feeding*".[301] It expressed the act of bringing the mouth to the food, like a mother brings her baby to her breast for nursing (fig. 32). Considering the fact that the inscription is above the altar with food, it would be more logical to go with the translation of feeding. So both the mourner and the embalmer would be feeding (and therefore giving life to) the dead. With this information and thanks to the main four elements, this entire scene can be re-interpreted in a more detailed way. Below, I will first give a description of the scenes and then reinterpret their meaning:

1. The scene takes place during the funerary ceremony, so the main subject was the deceased. He was considered to be the newly born in Ancient Egyptian belief. His revival was a new birth, so the mummy became a foetus in the womb and returned to life after the whole gestation. After that, his first food would be breast milk. In this context the expression *ḏꜣt rꜣ* would be full of meaning if we link it to the gesture of taking the baby to a breast for nursing. So, the mummy (the new-born) would be having the first meal of his new life.

2. The *ḏrty*, or the two kites, were the representatives of Isis and Nephthys. Both played a very important role in a special mourning ritual: both shook and pulled their hair reliving again the episode of the myth of Osiris in which the corpse of the god was revived by Isis. In the scene of the tomb of Qar there is only one *ḏrt* mourner, who probably played the role of Isis. The moment of restoring the dead's body and his powers for returning to life is presented here.

3. The embalmer is a very important figure during the funerary procession. He was responsible for the mummification, which in the myth of Osiris was the role of Anubis. Once every limb of the god's body was collected, Anubis restored the mummy by assembling each part. Afterwards, Isis restored the vital powers with her magic and Osiris came back to life. So again, we see the moment of restoring the mummy, which would explain why the embalmer and the mourner (Anubis and Isis) are presented together.

---

300 Simpson, 1976, p.5.

301 *Wb* 4, 514.

4. The lector priest was always present at Ancient Egyptian funerals, reciting all sacred texts and leading the ceremony. Especially in the New Kingdom, the lector priest is always present on depictions, reciting his texts during the Opening of the Mouth Ceremony. In Qar's tomb he is the third member of the staff officiating during the rite.

← Fig. 32
Statuette of nursing woman. Giza. Dynasty V. Photo: Metropolitan Museum of Art of New York

5. We find the image of two tied-up oxen closing the register. It seems logical to assume just one ox was meant here, alive in the upper half and already dead in the lower one. The slaughtering of an ox is a funerary practice connected with the sacrifice of the Sethian victim; this rite was a reproduction of the death of Seth in the myth of Osiris.

All components of this scene refer to mythical practices performed in order to restore the corpse of Osiris and bring him back to life; the entire scene is supervised by the lector priest. All this happened during the Opening of the Mouth Ceremony, the main Ancient Egyptian rite for guaranteeing the resurrection of the dead of course. Therefore this small scene was very important in the decorative program of Qar's tomb; it had to be there to assure Qar's resurrection in the Afterlife. But the Egyptian artist in the Old Kingdom had to find a way of representing it in a discrete (even codified) fashion.

Taking a closer look at the inscriptions accompanying this depiction, the bottom register of the north wall is crucial for understanding the whole composition. The word identifying the building at the left end is *uabet*, which means "*pure and clean place*",[302] but not necessarily just "*embalming place*". The word uabet in the Middle Kingdom also meant "*tomb*".[303] Could it be translated as "*tomb*" in the Qar scene as well? If that is the case, the scene could have to be read in a different direction and order: not downwards, but upwards.[304] When considering this, the sequence would start at the right end of the lower register. The procession would move the coffin onto a boat, where the two professional mourners, the embalmer and the lector priest would accompany the corpse. The retinue would arrive at the uabet building, which could now be considered the burial place. In the upper register the artists represented what was happening inside the *uabet* building, the tomb. They did this with the three main figures for the ceremony: the lector priest, the embalmer and the professional mourner. And their presence allows us to divide the upper register into three scenes:

1. "The three (mourner, embalmer and lector priest) and the transportation of the coffin". That would be the retinue and the mummy reaching the tomb.

302 *Wb* I, p.284.

303 *Wb* I, p.284, IV.

304 In fact, it is not uncommon that Egyptian artists designed a decoration from bottom to top, as this was also the case with the Opening of the Mouth Ceremony in the tomb of Rekhmire.

2. "The three inside the *w3t*": This Egyptian word meant "*way*" or just "*a part of a place*".[305] According to the image and the hieroglyphs, inside the *w3t* were several elements that can help us understand its function:

The tools of the *ḥmt* (artisans)
The tools of the lector priest;
Everything necessary for the purification of the food[306]. This should refer to the final food offerings;
The icon shows that in this *w3t* there is water.

These four points reflect what the retinue needed for the Opening of the Mouth Ceremony, as we can see in many scenes from tombs and *papyri* of the New Kingdom.

3. "The three during the *ḏ3t r3* and the slaughter of the ox": We have already seen that this image could be a way of representing the Opening of the Mouth Ceremony.

In conclusion, the decoration on the north wall in the tomb of Qar should be read from bottom to top. The artist would have narrated the arrival of the funerary procession at the tomb, the resurrection rites practiced on the mummy and, as a consequence at the very top of the wall, Qar finally sits revitalised in front of his funerary offerings. This analysis of the whole composition demonstrates that the Opening of the Mouth Ceremony and the mourning rite executed by the professional mourners was something performed inside the tomb and out of sight. Meanwhile, the rest of the members of the procession would stay outside waiting until the team of "restorers" would finish their work.

5.2.5.3. The ostracon 5886 in the Manchester museum.

Not only large scenes on walls of great tombs can provide valuable information, small quotidian objects can also be very useful for the understanding of the Ancient Egyptian funerary rituals. This is the case with the Ostracon 5886 from Manchester Museum, found in Thebes and dating to the New Kingdom (fig. 33). An Egyptian artist drew an ink sketch on it, depicting a scene of an Egyptian burial. The plan of the tomb is seen from a bird's-eye perspective, while the members of the funerary company and the coffin are shown from a frontal view.[307] Outside the tomb a group of four mourners is standing while weeping. Next to them, a priest is burning incense and pouring water. Although it is not very clear, it seems that the artist intended to draw the woman on the right with a lock of hair falling in front of her face. In contrast, it should be pointed out that while the three others appear with their arms raised, the mourner with the hair falling onto her face has her arms hanging down.

Egyptian artists used a very similar solution in the tomb of Rekhmire (TT100) (fig. 2), where some mourners are kneeling with their head in their hands, some others are stand-

305 *Wb* I, p.248, II.

306 This inscription deserves special attention, because it is unclear. It seems to refer to purification (*abu*) of the "*feeding*" (*ḏ3t r3*).

307 The combination of different visual perspectives was common in ancient Egyptian art.

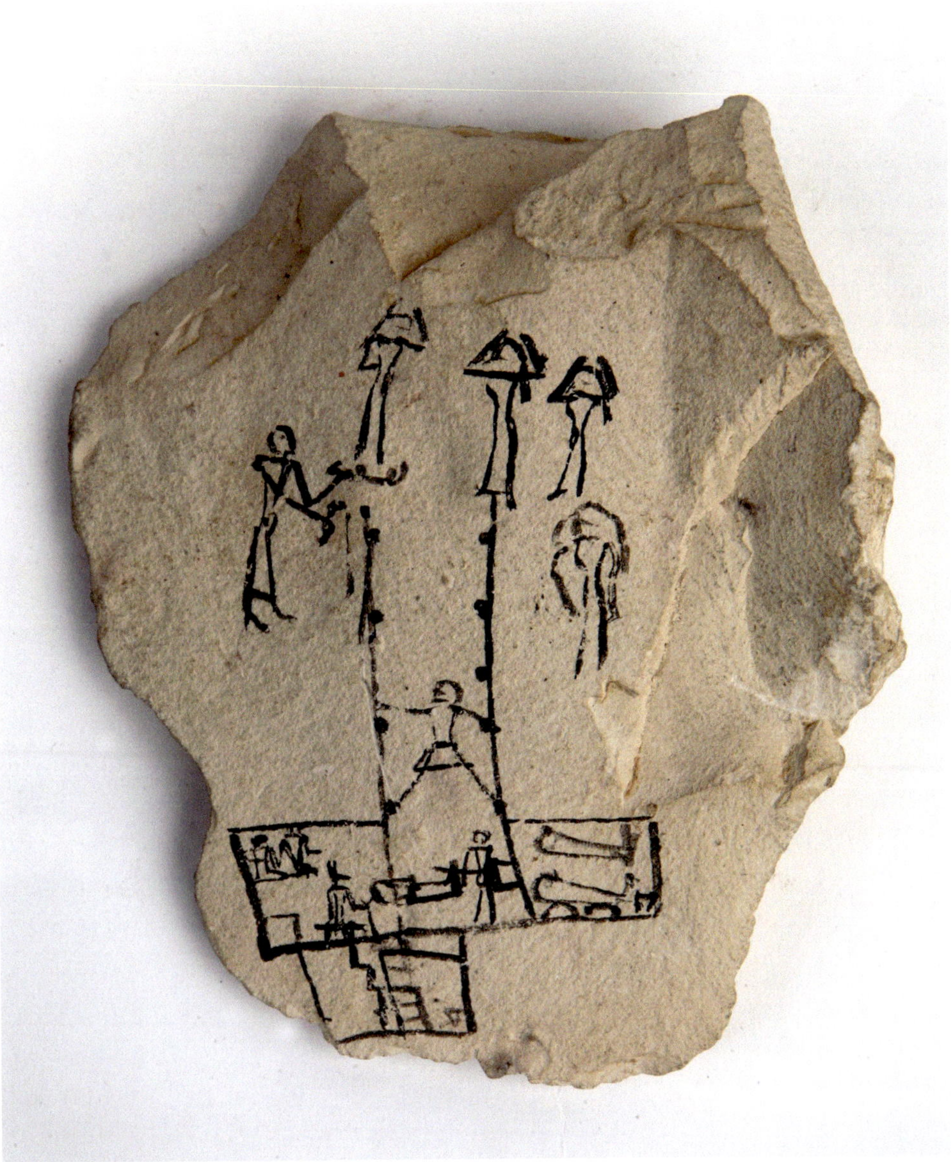

← Fig. 33
Ostracon of limestone with a scene of a funeral. Thebes. New Kingdom. Manchester Museum, acc. No. 5886. Photo: ©Manchester Museum, University of Manchester.

ing with their arms crossed over their chests and another one is standing with crossed arms as well, but with the mane of hair covering her face. Furthermore, in the tomb of Amenemhat (TT82) we can see a group of common mourners, some with their arms raised, some covering their faces with their hands and two making the *nwn* gesture of shaking the hair forwards. Near them, a priest holds an incense burner and a purifying water vessel, the same feature as on the *ostracon* in the Manchester Museum.

The artist of the *ostracon* sketched a man descending into the tomb and another one in the funerary chamber carrying the coffin. However, the most important people are a man with a jackal head next to the corpse and two kneeling figures in a corner of the chamber. The scene seems to depict the very moment when the coffin was placed inside the tomb. But were the man with a jackal-headed mask and those two kneeling figures necessary for placing the coffin inside the tomb or did they serve another purpose in the sketch?

The schematic scene most likely represented what happened inside the tomb in order to revive the deceased. It seems that before putting the mummy into his final burial place, first the Opening of the Mouth Ceremony took place inside the tomb. That would explain the presence of the man with the jackal-headed mask as a living image of Anubis playing the role of the embalmer. In my opinion, the two kneeling figures would be the two mourners in the role of Isis and Nephthys, who performed the professional mourning rite in favour of the mummy. So, the three formed the trio of the common Egyptian iconography in which Anubis assists the mummy, while Isis and Nephthys are (standing or kneeling) at both ends of the corpse. The *ostracon* seems to reflect an actual moment of an Ancient Egyptian burial, with these two women apart in the chamber standing still, seemingly without performing any activity.

The man to the right of the mummy is holding a long straight object, which seems to be more similar to a kind of club or a stick. Could this perhaps be the adze used in the Opening of the Mouth Ceremony? If so, the man holding the instrument would be a *sem* priest. Or could he be holding a papyrus roll? In the latter case he would be a lector priest reciting the sacred texts. Both hypotheses seem quite tempting, but we cannot confirm them. In any case, both men are in that moment holding the mummy as if they want to position it down into the shaft, as if the restoring rites of the Opening of the Mouth Ceremony have been finished. It does not seem too far-fetched to think that such schematic drawing would represent the end of the funeral; the Opening of the Mouth Ceremony had been concluded, and for that reason the two professional mourners would be kneeling, and the two priests would be placing the mummy into his final burial place. Meanwhile, outside the tomb, the group of common mourners would be lamenting, three of them with their arms raised and one of them with hair over her face and her arms hanging down.

Summed up, the *nwn* and *nwn m* gesture had two components, with different meanings and taking place in different moments of the funerary ceremony, a public element and a private element.

The public one made outdoors by common mourners during the procession, or outside the tomb in the necropolis. In this case the *nwn/nwn m* gesture would be related to the chaos, the darkness of the death and would be a sign of despair. The dishevelled hair of the common mourners would be a symbol of the primeval moment, when the chaos dominated the world and every creative principle, still without activity, was in the primordial waters of the *Nwn*. The hair over their faces would cover their eyes, this way evoking the darkness of death and also of the primordial waters.

And then there is the private element of the funerary, conducted indoors, carried out by the two women in the divine role of Isis and Nephthys in the ritual process of resurrecting of the dead. In this case, the same practice had a regenerating objective. The two professional mourners went into the tomb and played the role of Isis and Nephthys. They performed a professional mourning rite, which was based on the myth of Osiris. Shaking and/or pulling their hair forwards to the mummy, they symbolized the divine lament in which Isis, as a kite, blew air into Osiris' nostrils by flapping her wings, and gave him back his virility by putting herself over his phallus. This mourning rite was just one of several practices, which together formed the Opening of the Mouth Ceremony and which were performed out of sight from the rest of the members of the procession.

PART II | **Shaking and Pulling hair**

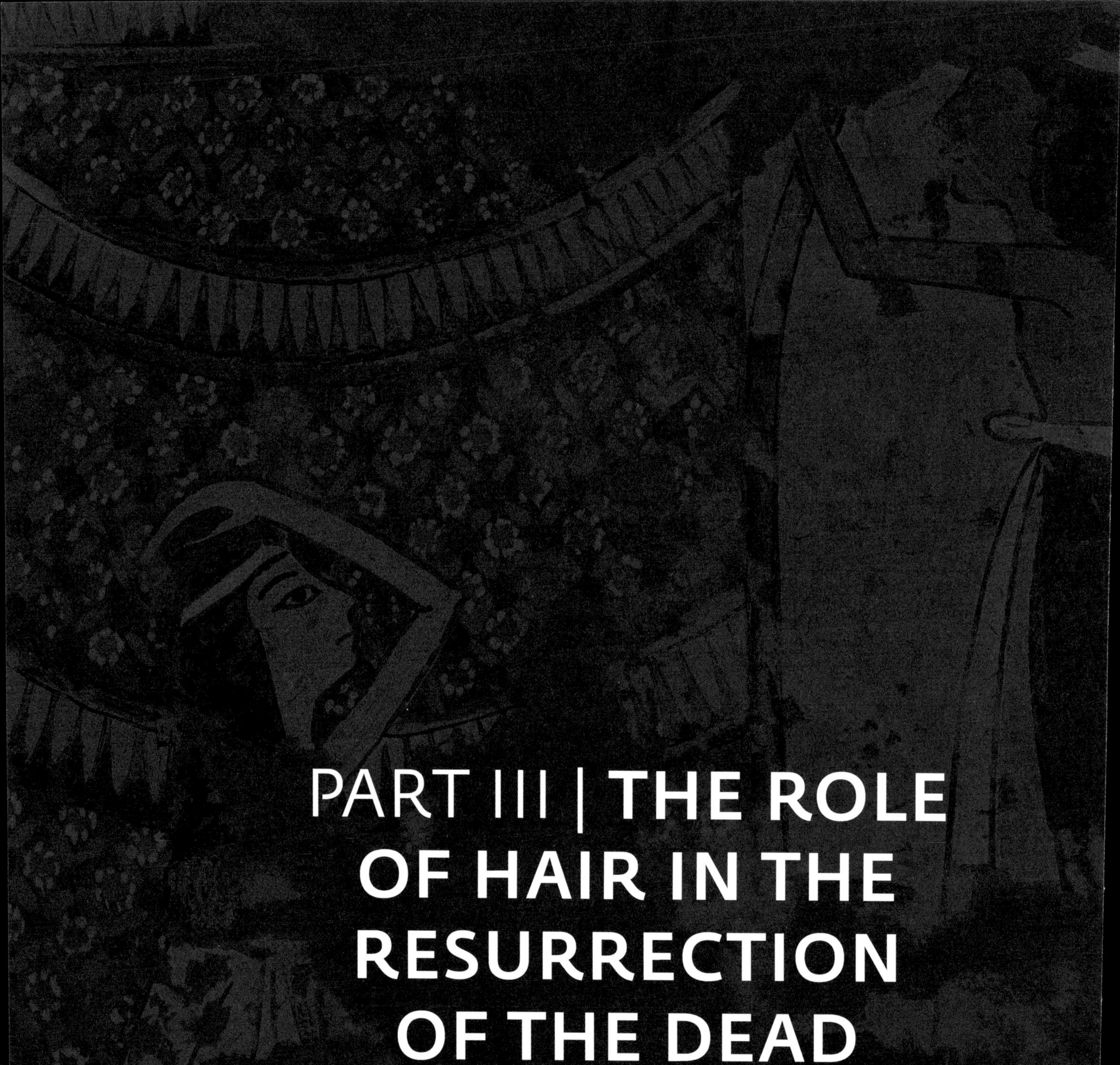

PART III | THE ROLE OF HAIR IN THE RESURRECTION OF THE DEAD

In many scenes depicting funerary processions in private Theban tombs from the New Kingdom, the two mourners in the role of Isis and Nephthys were depicted with long hair, standing on either sides of the coffin during the procession (fig. 8). In the same tombs, the two *ḏrtyt* appeared at the end of the funerary ceremony with short hair offering the *nw* vases to the four pools (fig. 7). The image of the professional mourner with short hair was also common in earlier periods of Egyptian history, as can also be found in the tombs of Qar and Idu at Giza from the Old Kingdom (fig. 31) or in the tomb of Antefoker at Thebes from the Middle Kingdom. In all these early cases, the two *ḏrty* already appear with short hair during the funerary procession, accompanying the coffin. The long hair of the two professional mourners was very important in Ancient Egyptian funerals to guarantee the dead's resurrection. The reason for this was that the gesture of shaking (*nwn*) and/or pulling (*nwn m*) the long mane of hair recalled the episode of the myth of Osiris in which the god was "awakened" by Isis with the assistance of Nephthys. Why would those two women be represented with short hair then? Additional information is that especially the images from the New Kingdom show the two *ḏrty* without a mane of hair at the end of the funerary ceremony, that is, when they had already performed their mourning rite and the resurrection had become a fact.

According to the myth, Osiris's rebirth happened just after Horus had fought against Seth, the murderer of Osiris, when he could avenge his father's death. In the course of this battle, Horus lost his eye. Once he had won the battle, he also regained his eye, which was healed with the aid of the god Thoth. The recovered eye was the Udjat eye, the lunar eye, the symbol of the full moon, a symbol of recovery. Horus then offered the Udjat eye to his father Osiris to help him with his final resurrection in the Hereafter. If the mourning rite made by the two professional mourners was a way of reproducing the myth in a symbolic manner, it is hypothetically possible that the rebirth of the corpse after the official lament and the two *ḏrty* with the short hair were also linked to the end of the legend of Osiris and that they also had something to do with Horus and the Udjat eye. The question is then whether there was a relationship between hair and the lunar eye in Egyptian belief. In the following paragraphs we will go into this connection of hair and the Udjat in more detail.

1. The hair *smꜣ* and the healing of the lunar eye

We have seen how the reading of the *Coffin Texts* shows us many different aspects of hair, related to restoring practices or regenerating symbols. One important and basic symbol of restoration in Egyptian religion is the Udjat eye; the eye of Horus, injured during the fight against Seth, which was identified with the moon. The process of waxing from crescent to full moon was assimilated with the combat between both gods. The full moon was evidence of the final victory of Horus over Osiris's murderer, completed with the resurrection of Osiris as king of the Hereafter. Many chapters of the *Coffin Texts* mention the hair, *smꜣ*, in this Osirian context of healing.

For instance, in Chapter 133 of the *Coffin Texts* we can read: *"Those ones who are in their temples they blink and make the Great One. The Great One belongs to me; the eye of the Great*

One belongs to me. I have spat[308] *over the hair, smꜣ, of Šw*[309] *for his healing (Iw psg.n.i smꜣ n Šw r nḏm.f).*[310] *Everything has been given to me, I feel triumphant, and I stand up triumphant. I have created all my family for whom I have spoken. I am Re, the sun's father."* And the same line in Chapter 164 of the *Coffin Texts* reads: *"...I treat the great god because of his harm, which one is the suffering of the great god? It is his head, his shoulder and his leg. I came to spit on his shoulder, for refreshing the hair, smꜣ, (skbb.i smꜣ)*[311]*...and for healing the two legs of the great god...."*

The parallel of the lunar eye and hair, *smꜣ*, seems evident from these two passages. In both cases, spitting over the hair is a gesture of recovery. Once the eye is healed, the deceased rises triumphantly and can be reborn. Chapter 164 also mentions some mutilations that have happened in the myth of Osiris and that have been healed after the battle; for that reason, the god spits over the injured shoulder first. According to P. Barguet, the passage relates the healing of Osiris's injured shoulder and hair, *smꜣ*, that is, the lunar eye.[312]

In Chapter 610 of the *Coffin Texts* the healing is done with the hair, *smꜣ*, of *Atum* and also for a deity named *Údd*: *"...this N. has spat over the hair, smꜣ, of ꜣtum, he has refreshed Údd (iw psg.n N pn smꜣ pn n (I)tmw ḳb.(n).f Údd.)*[313] *Shu and Thoth, beloved, being together behind the great god, Shu and the hair, smꜣ,... this N, has spat (over) the hair, smꜣ, this N has refreshed his vertebra. It is medicine inside the body of this N...*[314]*."* In Egyptian mythology the moon, i.e. the Udjat eye, is one of the eyes of *Atum*, the other one was the sun. *Údd* is a name deriving from the verb *hd*, which means "*to attack*",[315] and the meaning of *hdd* could be "*attacked*", "*the one who has been attacked*".[316] Consequently, *Údd* can be a personification of the attacked eye of Horus, hence the need to refresh it in order to cure it. It is also interesting to note how in Chapter 667 of the *Coffin Texts* the healing of the hair, *smꜣ*, is equivalent to offering a leg and giving breath: *"...He has spat (over) the hair, smꜣ, (psg.f smꜣ)*[317]*...he carries a leg and he gives breath to who does not have it. This N has brought his ba soul; he has taken his power and magic."* Let us remember that both gestures (offering an ox leg and giving breath) are two actions directly related to the Opening of the Mouth Ceremony, when the dead recovers his powers for his new life.[318]

Finally, we find a very visual description in all these processes of healing the damaged lunar eye in Chapter 335 of the *Coffin Texts*: *"...I have recovered the eye after it was dam-*

308 *iw sḏm.n.f* is a narrative tense, which stresses a very important fact of the story.

309 According to Barguet, it is the city of Seth in the Heracleopolitan nome (P. Barguet, 1986, p.256, n.6).

310 

311 

312 P. Barguet, 1986, p.377, n.10.

313 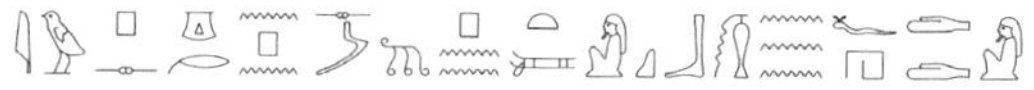

314 Healing properties of saliva.

315 *Wb* II, 504, 15.

316 It is a 2-lit. verb with second radical geminated in perfect passive participle.

317 

318 *Vide supra* p.65.

aged the night of the combat between the Two Fellows.[319] *I have raised the hair from the Udjat eye when he was furious (iw ṯs.n.ỉ šny m wḏꜣt m tr.s n nšnỉ).*[320] *Who raises the hair from the Udjat eye? Who is the Udjat eye in his moment of anger? It is the right eye of Re and Thoth is the one who raises the hair from it (ỉn grt ḏḥwty ṯs šn pn ỉm.s).*[321]*"* We read here about the action of "*raising the hair from the Udjat eye.*" P. Barguet suggested that the preposition *m* in the sentence had the meaning of "*as*", so according to him the translation should be: "*the hair, šny, was the same Udjat eye.*" However, if we translate the preposition *m* as "*from*", the passage makes more sense in this context. It would describe the gesture of moving the hair away from the eye in order to heal it, and also from the face to allow seeing the light after the darkness. The hair symbolising the harm to the eye is then eliminated, the healed eye becomes the *Udjat* eye as the image of the full moon and of resurrection.[322] In every chapter discussed here, we find a common denominator: the hair, mainly *smꜣ,* (but in one case also *šny*[323]), is somehow linked to the *Udjat* eye. It is also important to remember that the Eye of Horus, offered to Osiris, was considered to be poured water[324] and the connection of hair with water related to resurrection is already clear to us. Therefore, it seems reasonable to consider a relationship between hair and the *Udjat eye* as well.

This hair/eye gets involved in the fight, suffers damage and is treated and healed with the saliva. The link to the myth of Osiris is evidently the moment in which the eye of Horus needs to be healed by Thoth. We have not yet reached rebirth, but it is the instant just before that, when Horus has vanquished Seth, but the final victory is still one step away: recovering the lunar eye. Spitting over the hair belongs to the process of creating the *Udjat* eye.

The belief that the god Thoth is the one who healed the injured eye of Horus with some sputum already appears in Egyptian mythology in the Old Kingdom: "*He has come with that one that spits the hair (smꜣ), for his hair (smꜣ), which is sick at the beginning of each month and sick*[325] *at the beginning of middle month*".[326] This passage belongs to a chapter of the *Pyramid Texts*, which mentions two lunar celebrations: *ỉbd*[327] (the second day of the month) and *smdt*[328] (the fifteenth day of the month). They were Heliopolitan celebrations, which included some rites for the reconstruction of the lunar eye, with the

319 Horus and Seth.

320 

321 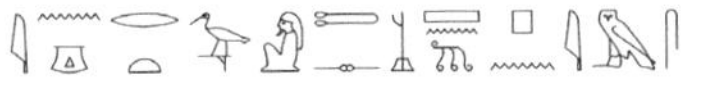

322 Actually, the meaning of this gesture is similar to another mentioning in Chapter 533 of the *Coffin Texts*, where the face of Hathor becomes visible and clears, after separating her two lateral ringlets, opening them as if they were curtains through which the deceased can see the full moon (Valdesogo, 2005, p.58)

323 According to H. Kees, *šnỉ* and *smꜣ* both have the same relationship with the lunar legend (Kees, 1925, p.8).

324 *Vide supra* p. 24.

325 The text uses the Egyptian word *nḳm*, parallel to "*sick*", which actually designates a "*bad property of the hair*" (*Wb* II, 344, 3).

326 *Pyr.*, 521.

327 *Wb* I, 65, 10. *ỉbd/ꜣbd* was also the Egyptian word for "*month*".

328 The ancient form of *nt*, the lunar festival of the fifteenth day of the month (*Wb* IV, 147, 1).

purpose of returning it to health.[329]

These lunar festivals also appear in chapters of the *Coffin Texts,* in which the deceased has to be transformed into Thoth and has to perform some lunar practices: *"...this N. is the one who makes the rite ibd and he is the one who controls the rite nt. The plait of hair of Horus is on the hand of this N. in Thoth's entourage (iw dnt irt ¡r ḥr(y)-ˁ n N pn m smswt ḏḥwty) ..."*.[330] At this point it is important to remember Chapters 167 and 674 of the *Coffin Texts*, which mention the preparation of the mourner's hair, *smꜣ*, together with two lunar celebrations[331]: *snwt*[332] (the sixth day of the month) and *dnit*[333] (the seventh and twenty-third day of the month[334]).

Healing the lunar eye is an action full of symbolism because the eye, as the visual organ, is a metaphor for light and its disappearance or mutilation is a synonym for darkness. The sacrifice of the eye and its following recovery supposes a regenerating act, equivalent to "creation after the chaos". Restitution of vision means access to light after the darkness of death. In the religious texts, this healing is achieved by moving the hair away from the eye. And the one who moves the hair away from the eye is Thoth, because, according to the legend, he is the lunar god who heals the eye of Horus after the fight against Seth.

If Thoth spits over the hair, *smꜣ*, in order to heal the eye, this cannot be the healthy eye, but has to be the damaged eye of Horus, which in Egyptian is *nknkt*[335] or *nkkt*[336] and which needs a cure in order to become the Udjat eye. Once again, we find the hair, *smꜣ*, with a negative connotation; we have previously seen that the hair, *smꜣ*, was a symbol of chaos, the primordial waters; it was the *Nun* that dominated the world before the final creation.[337] H. Kees already considered that the hair, *smꜣ*, in the context that we are talking about here, could be the damage suffered by the lunar eye,[338] which creates the darkness of the night, in the same way that the hair, *smꜣ*, over the faces of the mourners covers their eyes, blocking their vision. So, spitting over the hair, *smꜣ*, would eliminate that damage, in the same way that moving the hair away from the face allows the light to be seen.

The hair, *smꜣ*, over the mourners' faces would then symbolize the disorder dominating the fight between Horus and Seth. This combat is full of meaning, since according to J.E. Cirlot the fight is the "primeval sacrifice"[339]; it is the combat between two opposite forces

329 S. Ratié, 1984, p.179.

330 *CT* IV, 277.

331 *Vide supra* p.22.

332 *Wb* IV, 153, 4.

333 *Wb* V,465, 6 and 7.

334 Lull, 2006, p.91.

335 *Wb* II, 347, 6.

336 *Wb* II, 347, 9.

337 *Vide supra* p.23.

338 H. Kees, 1925, p.8.

339 J. E. Cirlot, 1991, p.282.

and it contributes to stimulating the vital energy, with the result of the victory of order over chaos. This victory means the creation of the world, and the winner emerges from it as a hero with additional powers. In the funerary context that meant the recovery of the Udjat eye and access to light, the resurrection of the deceased and the beginning of his new life.

2. The hair *sꜣmt* and the Udjat eye

Once the damaged eye of Horus is healed, it becomes the Udjat eye, the full moon as a symbol of complete regeneration. It is the final act of the myth of Osiris, when he is reborn and becomes triumphant over his enemies; on earth this signifies the deceased's resurrection at the end of the funeral.

Religious documents seem to show a connection between the Udjat eye to a hair element called *sꜣmt* and some chapters of the *Coffin Texts* mention this *sꜣmt* and the shaving of the mourners related to this final episode of the myth. In this moment of Osiris's victory over his enemies and his resurrection, Chapter 339 of the *Coffin Texts* reads: "*...Busiris, this is the day of giving the Udjat eye to his lord. Pe-Dep,*[340] *this is the day of shaving the mourners (P-Dp hrw pw n ẖꜥḳ iꜣkbywt)*[341]*...*" This passage has three interesting points: it mentions some towns related in some manner to Osiris and his burial;[342] Thoth is the god claiming "true of voice" of Osiris; and Horus offers his Udjat eye to his father.[343] This last act of the son culminates in the final resurrection. It means the end of the chaos, the restitution of order and the beginning of the new life. Osiris is reborn as king of the Hereafter, while Horus inherits the throne on earth. And, according to Chapter 339 of the *Coffin Texts*, this moment of restoration is the moment of shaving the mourners in Buto, in other words shaving Isis and Nephthys.

Chapter 942 of the *Coffin Texts* is too fragmentary, but it is clear that it alludes to the fight between Horus and Seth:"*Provide with her sꜣmt burning (?) (ẖtm m sꜣmt.s nbi*[344]*)... ...those ones from Hermopolis adore him*[345]*(...), they break the double power. My coming up is the coming up of this goddess, rising with Re... the only lord, which has taken the flame of the Luminous One. The two iꜣrty of Sokaris*[346] *are shaved for her (ẖꜥk n.s iꜣrty %kr).*[347] *The face is adorned* [348]*(...) made against her in the name of Wnwt.*[349] *Seth is put by her under her pleats*

340 Buto.

341 

342 Busiris (the place of Osiris' spine), Letopolis (the place of his shoulder), Buto (where Isis and Nephthys came from), Abydos (his burial place)

343 The offering of the Udjat eye will be the offering par excellence, so everything offered will be called "the eye of Horus" (A. Erman, 1952, p.209).

344 

345 Reconstruction could be (*n*).*f*.

346 In ancient Egypt there was an assimilation between Osiris and Sokaris.

347 

348 Or "*dressed*".

349 Name related to the *uraeus* (*Wb* I, 317, 11).

(...) the peace is made (...) in their names. I am alive and intact, they are alive and intact."

Let's have a look at the hair elements we find in the text. P. Barguet translated the first sentence as: "*her plait is destroyed*". In fact, the verb *ḥtm* can be translated as "*destroy*"[350], but the meaning of the sentence remains obscure. There is another verb *ḥtm* with a different determinative which could be translated as "*to provide with*", "*to equip with*", and specially "*to equip the face with the eye*".[351] So maybe we could consider the sentence to be an expression related to the recovered eye, the Udjat eye. Therefore we can now read "*the face is adorned*". Regarding the word *iꜣrty* two main points should be underlined: the dual form and the hair determinative. This, and the mention of Buto in Chapter 339 of the *Coffin Texts* remind us of the two mourners Isis and Nephthys. The Egyptian word *iꜣr* means "*sadness*" or "*mourning*".[352] R.O. Faulkner translated the term *iꜣrr* as "*weakness of the eye*" or "*weakness of the heart*"[353]; *iꜣrt* is also an Egyptian expression that designates the *uraeus* of Re.[354] We could also consider that the *iꜣrty* of Chapter 942 of the *Coffin Texts* would be the two *uraei* of Sokaris (a god assimilated to Osiris), which had to be cut. However, the meaning of *ẖꜥḳ* means "*to shave*"[355] and it is a term applied only to hair. So, Chapter 942 mentions the shaving of two locks or pieces of hair, *iꜣrty*. With these *iꜣrty* of Sokaris we may be encountering another case of metonymy,[356] in which the two mourners are mentioned by their most relevant part. The *iꜣrty* are actually a way of describing Isis and Nephthys, so here we are actually reading about the shaving of both mourners' locks of hair.

After shaving the *iꜣrty,* the text explains how the face is adorned or dressed, but with what? Should we consider the arrangement of the Udjat eye on Osiris/the deceased's face? That would be reflecting the final episode of the myth and it would fit in perfectly with the end of the chapter. When Seth is put under *Wnwt*, which is related to the *uraeus*, peace is made because in Egyptian belief the *uraeus* is a benefactor; it eliminates the evil (Seth), it helps to restore universal order. We can thus conclude that there is a direct relationship between the Udjat eye offer to Osiris, the final resurrection and the shaving of the two mourners.

In Chapter 1131 of the *Coffin Texts* the dead is described as an image of Osiris. In this context the deceased goes ahead to his resurrection, but before that, something else must happen: *"The sꜣmt is cut; the eye is sealed by the nestling in its hole (ḥdḳ sꜣmt irt ẖtmt(i) n ṯꜣ n bꜣbꜣ.f). "*[357] P. Barguet[358] and William A. Ward[359] transliterated this sentence as fol-

---

350 *Wb* III, 197.

351 *Wb* III, 196, 14.

352 *Wb* I, 32, 2.

353 R.O. Faulkner, 1962, p.9, 5.

354 *Wb* I, 32, 3.

355 *Wb* III, 365.

356 *Vide supra* p.48.

357 

358 P. Barguet, 1986, p.665.

359 W.A. Ward, 1975, p.62.

lows: *ḥdḳ sꜣmt ỉrt ḫtmt n tꜣ nbꜣbꜣ.f*, with a verb (*nbꜣbꜣ*) and an unclear translation.[360] By changing the end of the sentence to *tꜣ n bꜣbꜣ.f*, the text makes more sense: "*the nestling tꜣ*[361] *is into its hole bꜣbꜣ*". The word *bꜣbꜣ* can refer to the seven facial orifices, two of which are the eye sockets.[362] Taking into consideration our context, it seems rather logical to think of *bꜣbꜣ* in this chapter as a way of referring to the eye socket. That allows us to translate the sentence as "*the eye is sealed (or closed)*", since the nestling is inside the orbit (as a nest) and impedes the vision. This would be a metaphor of the blindness caused by death and which Osiris got out of once the Udjat eye was restored.

We also need to focus on a subsequent sentence at the end of the chapter that reads: "*Live the nestling that goes out from you... flies the flight and live Osiris...*" This flight is strongly connected with the resurrection of the Osiris-bird. When the nestling remains inside the nest-socket, the eye is closed (which means no access to light) it is the moment of shadows and darkness (death). Chapter 1131 of the *Coffin Texts* connects that concept to the cutting of the *sꜣmt*, after that the nestling flies and the eye can open. It symbolizes the capacity to see, the brightness after darkness, Osiris/the deceased's return to life. This idea of resurrection through a flight dates back to the Old Kingdom: the dead king could reach the Hereafter as the eye of Horus, but he was usually transformed into a bird, using the powers of this animal to fly upwards.[363]

Summed up, the main ideas about the funerary rites that we can gain from these three chapters of the *Coffin Texts* are:

1. The hair element *sꜣmt* is cut just before the final resurrection.
2. Osiris's resurrection is connected with the shaving of the two mourners.
3. The cutting of the *sꜣmt* is connected with the restoration of the *Udjat* eye and the recovery of vision.

I will now further discuss the three variables related to the *sꜣmt*: the mourning rite, the hair and the cutting of it.

2.1 The word *sꜣmt*: "mourning rite"

If the *sꜣmt* had to be shaven off, it seems quite obvious that this word represented a hair element. However, the Egyptian term *sꜣmt* was more flexible and had different meanings.[364] The generic meaning of *sꜣmt* was "*sadness*", [365] but it could also mean "*moan*" [366]

360 It seems to be a verb related to the eye of Horus (*Wb* II, 243, 14), but the meaning remains unclear.

361  this sign is the image of the nestling in the nest 

362 *Wb* I, 419, 1.

363 *Pyr.*, 1216 y 1770. Whitney M. Davies, 1977, p.167.

364 In the Old Kingdom *sꜣmt* is documented as a personal name (P. Kaplony, 1966, p.68)

365 *Wb* IV, 18, 10.

366 D. Meeks, 1977-1979, p.306, nº 78.3295.

or "*mourning*".[367] Some scholars have translated *sꜣmt* as "*lock of hair*" [368] and according to some others it could describe "*hair not cut*" as a sign of mourning[369] or "*careless hair*".[370] William A. Ward, on the basis of Chapter 1131 of the *Coffin Texts*, concludes that the expression *ḥdḳ sꜣmt* meant "*cut the dishevelled hair*"[371] and he refers to the *Prophecy of Neferty* for arriving at this interpretation.[372] This manuscript relates how the wise man Neferty tells Pharaoh Snofru in Dynasty IV about the future (First Intermediate Period) as a chaotic time where all rules and systems, both natural and cultural, will become reversed. In Prophecy IX Neferty predicts that Egypt will be attacked by Asiatics, the sun will not shine, the Nile will dry up, there will be wars, etc., and among all those disasters he says that *"...nobody will cry for the dead, nobody will fast for the dead, a man's heart will be concerned just with himself, today will*[373] *not be any sꜣmt carried out (nn ìr.tw sꜣmt min),*[374] *the heart will be completely away from it..."*

There are different interpretations for this passage. W. Helck translated it as: "*...today no one will dress the mourning hairstyle*"; M. Lichtheim states that Neferty meant that mourning would not be done at all;[375] and for G. Lefebvre Neferty's words state that *"... there will not be mourning ceremonies...."*[376]

In my opinion, Neferty was predicting that nobody would cry nor fast for the dead, or do the *sꜣmt*. In other words, no one would perform the orthodox funerary practices. That means that *sꜣmt* was an Egyptian word for "*mourning*" as a funerary custom. In fact, thanks to some stele's found in the Serapeum at Saqqara, we know that during the embalming of the Apis bull there was a mourning ceremony called *sꜣmt*: "*... I was among the miserable, being in moaning, being in mourning.*[377] If this sentence was to be translated as *"...today the sꜣmt will not be carried out..."* it would match the chaotic situation Neferty was describing perfectly. In other words, everything points to the fact that the Egyptian word *sꜣmt* was a funerary custom related to hair and mourning. However, nothing indicates that it is referring to a specific hairstyle.

2.2 The word *sꜣmt*: "Hair"

The dead, as a newborn, is the son par excellence. For that reason, in Chapter 334 of the

367 D. Meeks, 1977-1979, p.304, n° 77.3349. Another way of writing *sꜣmt* was with the determinative of the crying eye .

368 R.O. Faulkner, 1962, p.210.

369 D. Meeks, 1977-1979, p.239, n° 79.2409.

370 D. Meeks, 1977-1979, p.304, n° 77.3349.

371 Ward, 1975, p.62, n.17.

372 W. Helck, 1970.

373 *nn sḏm.f* implies future.

374 

375 Lichtheim 1973, p.142.

376 G. Lefebvre, 1988, pp.101-102.

377 W. Jansen, 1994, p.35; J. Vercoutter, 1962, pp.37-38.

Coffin Texts, the deceased is the descendant of many gods; he is Ihy,[378] the son of Hathor,[379] the son of Re, of Isis, of Nephthys and he is Khonsu, as the lunar child[380]: *"To change into Ihy...I am the first product of Re, he created me in the body of my mother Isis... I am the son of Nephthys, I have been great and lucky. My sꜣmt is not destroyed in the bosom of my father and my mother (n htm n sꜣmt.i m ẖt i͗t.(i͗) mwt.(i͗)).*[381] *I live, I exist... I am a protector. I am ac-*

← Fig. 34
Khonsu with his lateral lock of hair. Relief from the funerary temple of Seti I in Dra Abu el-Naga. Thebes. Dynasty XIX. Photo: Mª Rosa Valdesogo.

claimed in my name of Khonsu. I am immortal in the sky, with Re and my mother Hathor...." The lunar nature of the dead comes from his condition as son of Re; he succeeds his father the sun who rules the daily sky; the moonlight follows the sunlight. The moon is also a symbol of new life in the Hereafter. The deceased exists and is acclaimed in the name of Khonsu. This god was the son of Amon and Mut (Theban Triad) and his image is characterised by the lunar headdress and the side lock of hair[382] (fig. 34). Khonsu and his side lock were a symbol of youth and showed him as the heir.[383] According to the passage, the *sꜣmt* has not been destroyed, the dead lives and exists afterwards. Could we think of the *sꜣmt* as the side lock of Khonsu?

If the lock of hair is synonymous with rebirth and inheritance, then the designation undestroyed would mean continuity and constant renovation. In the funerary thought of Ancient Egypt, the deceased could be assimilated to Khonsu as the first step of regeneration. This god with the side lock (maybe *sꜣmt*) is an image of the lunar crescent, the childhood of the moon. Khonsu starts its way to maturity, its growth in becoming the

378 He is the musician with the *sistrum*.

379 Already in the Old Kingdom the deceased is "*Horus, son of Osiris, ...son of Hathor, the semen of Geb*" (*Pyr.*, 466 a-b).

380 In fact, many passages of the text refer to the dead as a being in the middle of his first steps of existence.

381 

382 J. Zandee, referring to Kees, who considered the lunar eye a parallel to the lock of hair (*ZÄS* 60), identified this one with Khonsu (J. Zandee, 1953, p.112).

383 Ph. Derchain, 1962, p.40.

full moon, which materializes in the deceased's resurrection.[384] In this context it would make sense to translate the word *sꜣmt* as "*lock of hair*".

Chapter 334 of the *Coffin Texts* also mentions the gestation process of the dead: "*I am the ejaculated one, I passed through her two legs... I have germinated in the egg, I have harried up through its sf,*[385] *and I have slid on its snf.*[386] *I am the lord of the blood... my mother Isis conceives me when she is unaware of her body under the fingers of the lord of the gods, who invades her that day of magnificence... that day of disorder*[387]*....*" So, to keep the *sꜣmt,* meant to germinate in the egg. This is a vital centre which contains the energy to create a new being. The deceased remains unborn inside an imaginary egg, from where he will be reborn. The union of the lock of hair, *sꜣmt*, and the moment of rebirth/regeneration would show that the lock of hair, *sꜣmt*, is a vital factor which helps the deceased with his resurrection.

The *Coffin Texts* also mention the word *sꜣmt* not just as a symbolic factor but also as a physical element being manipulated and cut during the ceremony. For instance, Chapter 532 is about a Heliopolitan practice for restoring many parts of the corpse (head, eyes, neck and spine): "*Formula for placing the head... My head is placed. My neck is put by Tefnut. This is the day of putting their heads to the gods. My two eyes are given to me, I see with them. I have received my dorsal spine from Ptah-Sokaris. It is tied to me a lock of hair in Heliopolis, the day of cutting the sAmt (ṯs(w) n.ỉ syt m 'Iwnw hrw pw n ḥsḳ sꜣmt)*[388]" The most interesting point here is that, in order to restore the corpse, the *sꜣmt* is cut and a lock of hair *syt* is tied, the latter – as we have already seen – was a lock of hair depicted on mourners. So, again mourners' hair and restoration appear at the same moment.

At this point, we might look at the Osirian texts for a similar practices. The *Stundenwachen*-liturgy is a text known from inscriptions in Greco-Roman temples.[389] It tells about an Osirian ritual, which represents the life, death and resurrection of Osiris. In this ceremony, a practice of tying up a lock of hair is documented, and the two mourners personifying Isis and Nephthys played an important role in it. According to the inscription, in the second hour of the night, one of the mourners (the "small *ḏrt*") said: "*Join the head for you, put the plaits of hair" (ṯs n.k tp ḥm st ḫnkswt nw srt).*[390] The action takes place in a resurrection rite where the mourner is giving to Osiris a hair element. Could we think of a relationship between this passage of the *Stundenwachen* and Chapter 532 of the *Coffin*

384 In chapter 310 of the *Coffin Texts* there are many verbs related to growth, and that could be evidence of how the power of Khonsu increases (J. Zandee, 1953, p.111).

385 P. Barguet translates the word *sf* as "*egg white*".

386 P. Barguet translates the word *snf* as "*yolk*", although its real meaning is "*blood*".

387 The text employs the word *ḫnnw here*, which means "*uproar*", "*disturbance*" (*Wb* III, 383, 15). We are dealing with a moment of disorder here, during which the deceased is conceived; that would refer to the relationship we have already seen between chaos and orgy. So, this passage would be describing the required sexual act for the dead's rebirth.

388 

389 H. Junker studied the inscriptions from Dendera, Edfu and Philae.

390  H. Junker, 1910; E XIV, 95.

Texts? The imbalance is that the document of the Middle Kingdom mentions the lock of hair as *syt*, while the document from a later period mentions the plait of hair as *ḥnskwt nw srt*. The word *sr* can be translated as "*hair of a woman*" or "*hair of an animal*"[391] and *srt* means "*bull's hair*".[392] Should we think of this as a variation due to the passing of time?

Chapter 640 of the *Coffin Texts* also mentions the practice of cutting the *sꜣmt* in a Heliopolitan context: *"A knot is tied for me around me in the sky connected with the earth by Re each day. He puts a knot on the inert over his two thighs on that day of cutting the sꜣmt (smn.f ṯs(t) r nny(w) ḥr mnty.f hrw pwy (n) ḥsḳ sꜣmt)*[393]*...Seth ties a knot around me when the Ennead is in its first power, with no turmoil. You protect me against those who slew the father. Nut ties a knot around me, at the sight of the first time before I had seen Maat, before the gods were created.*[394] *I am Penty;*[395] *I am the heir of the gods."*

In any case, it seems that "to cut the *sꜣmt*" is a Heliopolitan rite,[396] as the lunar festivals we discussed in the previous chapter, which seems to be an important practice for the new life of the deceased. Could we think of cutting the *sꜣmt* in Chapters 532 and 640 of the *Coffin Texts* as a Heliopolitan rite with a lunar origin? In a symbolic context, cutting the *sꜣmt* was done when the moon was not a crescent anymore, but a full moon, so when the moon stopped being a child and became an adult. In the funerary ceremony, this cutting of the *sꜣmt* as a hair element was possibly done as a symbol of the lunar rebirth of the deceased; it could reflect the end of the chaos and darkness that dominated the universe before the creation. Cutting the *sꜣmt* would mean full moon, light, order and new life.

Cutting rituals (depilation, cutting hair, dental mutilations, etc.) occur in many cultures as one of the first acts of purification. This is how mankind distinguishes itself from animals.[397] The act of cutting is something fundamental in initiation ceremonies, like, for instance, circumcision.[398] We know that in Ancient Egypt the cutting of the side lock of children was done when they became adults, passing from childhood to a new social status (nowadays some African peoples still do the same).[399] It is for a good reason that Khonsu as the crescent lunar god is depicted with his side lock of hair. In this context

391 *Wb* IV, 191, 3 y 4.

392 *Wb* IV, 191, 5.

393 

394 The primeval moment.

395 *Pnt* is an Egyptian verb related to the making of bread (to knead) and beer (press) (*Wb* I, 511, 3). Desinence *-y* converts it into a prospective passive participle, which indicates a future fact, so, *Pnty* would mean "*The one who will be produced*"; that could refer to the deceased as a new creation.

396 P. Barguet, 1986, p.52, n.5

397 G. Durand, 1979, p.160.

398 Scholars consider that circumcision in Ancient Egypt was carried out between the ages of six and fourteen years.

399 In Roman times athletes and young men initiated in the Isis cult were recognizable because the former had a side lock on the top of the head, while the latter had it over the right ear; this lock of hair was cut around puberty at the same time as circumcision took place (V. von Gonzenbach, 1957 (summary in *AEB*, nº 57214, pp.61-62).

we may assume that the Egyptian action of cutting the *sꜣmt* (maybe a lock of hair) was a practice coming from very ancient times and adapted to different rites of passage:

CUTTING LOCK OF HAIR IN EGYPTIAN RITES OF PASSAGE

Common Life	Religious Sphere	Funerary Ceremony
Childhood→ Circumcision →Adulthood	Crescent/Khonsu with side lock of hair → Full Moon	Death→Mourning Rite→Resurrection

In fact, death for the Egyptians was a change of condition and a funerary ritual was not just a burial ceremony, but a rite of passage.[400] The dead changed his condition; he passed from dead to being reborn, he passed from child to adult, from crescent to full moon. During that process, the turning point was the cutting of the *sꜣmt*. Furthermore, the fact that the word *sꜣmt* can also be translated as "*mourning*" or "*sadness*" brings us back to the two professional mourning women and their hair. The word *sꜣmt* meant "*mourning*" as an official practice, but it was probably also related to the two professional mourners' hair. Was there a connection between these two mourners and the cutting of the *sꜣmt*? Following the order of appearance of the hair strands or elements in these texts, maybe the *smꜣ* was the shaken and dishevelled hair during the mourning rite, the hair assimilated to chaos and the damage done to the Horus eye, while the *sꜣmt* was the cut hair at the end of the mourning ceremony and related to the healthy Udjat eye, order and the deceased's resurrection.

2.3 Cutting the *sꜣmt*

Once the corpse of Osiris was restored, Horus gave him the Udjat eye, the healed lunar eye. With this offering, Horus assisted in the final reanimation of his father. It meant the lunar resurrection of Osiris, who became "*the lord of the Udjat eye*".[401] In the mythical sphere, the story culminates with Horus on the throne of Egypt and the resurrection of Osiris as king of the Hereafter, and in the funerary ritual this means the dead's rebirth. According to what we have read in the *Coffin Texts*, offering the Udjat eye, shaving the mourners in the role of Isis and Nephthys and cutting the *sꜣmt* happened at the end of the resurrection process done for the benefit of the deceased. But what can iconography tell us?

There are many examples in Egyptian art of the two professional mourners with short hair. From the Old Kingdom we have the funerary scenes in the tombs of Idu and Qar at Giza; although the funerary ceremony is not represented here in detail, in both cases the two *ḏrty* are depicted with short hair, standing at both ends of the coffin during the journey on the funerary boat to the tomb (fig. 31). In some wooden boat model from the Middle Kingdom, the Egyptian artisans depicted the two mourners accompanying the

---

400   Hays, 2013, p.170.

401   *Songs...*, 10, 3. For some scholars, the writing of Osiris's name means "*the place of the eye*" (W.B. Kristensen, 1992, p.17).

← Fig. 35
Wooden model of funerary boat. At both ends of the corpse the two professional mourners with shaven heads. Provenance unknown. Dynasty XII. London, British Museum, EA9524. Photo: © The Trustees of the British Museum.

corpse with short hair and sometimes even with evidence of a shaven head. This is the case with piece EA9524 in the British Museum, dating to Dynasty XII (fig. 35). This wooden model represents the funerary boat with the corpse and the two mourners at both ends. These two *ḏrty* are making a typical gesture of mourning, with their left arms raised and their hand on their head, while the right arms are extended towards the mummy. Both women's (and also the helmsman's) heads were painted with a pink colour and small black spots, indicating the scalp. In this way, the Egyptian artist indicated that their hair was very short or that their head had recently been shaven.

In this regard it is interesting to mention the tomb of Antefoker (TT60) at Thebes, dating to Dynasty XII, which has the most complete depiction of a funerary procession from the Middle Kingdom. On the south wall, the Egyptian artisan painted the journey to Abydos, the burial city of Osiris, and the *ḏrty* at both ends of the corpse appear with short hair (fig. 9). It is interesting to note that in many cases the colour of the hair is damaged or has disappeared completely, but it is possible to guess that it was black. However, the two heads of the two mourners were painted in a pink colour,[402] as if their heads had been shaven. In the New Kingdom tombs the Ancient Egyptian funeral was depicted with more detail and many of the reliefs and paintings in the tombs show some steps of the funerary ceremony. We can see the two *ḏrty* depicted with long hair while the procession was moving to the tomb. Having arrived there, the two professional mourners are depicted with short hair offering the *nw* vases to the four pools (fig. 7).[403]

↓ Fig. 36
Funerals from the tomb of Sobekmose in er-Rizeikat. The two professional mourners with no mane of hair facing the *mww* dancers. Drawing: Mª Rosa Valdesogo.

It seems that the short hair (or even a shaven head) could be a distinctive sign of the two professional mourners, like the metonymy we have seen before.[404] The tomb of Sobek-

402 Also the heads of *mww* dancers and the "man of Wet" (the embalmer?) receiving the boat were painted in a pink hue.

403 This scene can be seen in the tomb of of Pahery in el-Kab, Rekhmire in Gourna and Nefersekheru in Zawiyet el-Mayitin (all from Dynasty XVIII).In the tomb of Renni, also in el-Kab, there is an image of one *ḏrt* with short hair wrapping a person in a kind of cloth.

404 *Vide supra* p.48.

mose in el-Rizeikat (near Luxor), from the reign of Amenhotep III, gives us some clues about the final moment of the funeral and the recovery of the Udjat eye. On the north wall of the burial chamber there is a relief of the funerary procession (fig. 36).[405] On the right side we see the image of Anubis assisting the mummy while the coffin is pulled on a sledge by seven men. Just in front of these, and facing the *mww* dancers, are the two professional mourners without their manes of hair. Both *ḏrty* and *mww* are usually represented at the final moment of the funerary ceremony, and the procession ends with the image of Imenet, the goddess of the West. Above this scene there is a depiction of the deceased in front of the judges and the inscription reads: "*I am the nose that gives life to everybody on the day of completing the Udjat eye in Heliopolis (ink fnd pwy sꜥnḫ rḫyt nb hrw pwf n mḥ wḏꜣt m Ꞽwnw)*".[406] If, as we have read before, the day of giving the Udjat eye is the day of shaving the mourners, and the Heliopolitan practice of the cutting of the *sꜣmt* is related to the healing of the lunar eye, it is tempting to link the expression "*the day of cutting the sꜣmt*" from the *Coffin Texts* with "*the day of completing the Udjat eye*" from the tomb of Sobekmose and with the image of the two professional mourners with no mane of hair.

We have previously suggested the idea of cutting the lock of hair as a way of symbolizing the maturity of the moon (Udjat eye). And in this context, it is interesting to note that these three elements (hair, moon and Heliopolis) converge in Ancient Egypt from at least the Old Kingdom onwards with the figure of the girl *ḥwnt* .[407] According to the *Pyramid Texts* she is "*the great young who is in Heliopolis*"[408] and "*she gives or puts her two arms over the dead king*".[409] A. Erman and H. Grapow considered *ḥwnt wrt* to be a goddess in Heliopolis, who in the Late Period was assimilated to Hathor and Nephthys.[410] The *Pyramid Texts* also describe her as "*the little girl who is in the eye of Horus*",[411] in the pupil of the god's eye.[412] The hieroglyph of a youth with a lock of hair as determinative made H. Kees think of the lock of hair as a symbol and substitute for the lunar eye.[413] As a consequence, he considered the girl with the lock of hair to be the damaged eye of Horus, while the hair *smꜣ* was the damage itself.[414]

By extrapolation, we could also relate the shaving of the mourners to the images of the two *ḏrty* without a mane in the tombs of the New Kingdom mentioned earlier. Would

---

405 W.C. Hayes, 1939.

406 

407 The determinative shows the two typical features of childhood in Ancient Egypt: the finger in the mouth and the side lock of hair.

408 *Pyr.*, 728a.

409 *Pyr.*, 728a and 2002a.

410 *Wb* III, 53, 15,16 and 17.

411 *Pyr.*, 93.

412 *Wb* III, 53, 21.

413 H. Kees, 1925, p.6.

414 H. Kees, 1925, p.8. That also made H. Kees think that the lock of hair on the head of the bald of Heliopolis was related to the girl *ḥwnt* (H. Kees, 1925, p.6)

that also be linked to the cutting of the *s3mt*? If the word *s3mt* can be translated as "*lamentation*", it makes sense to assume that "to cut the *s3mt*", in addition of cutting the hair, could also be a way of referring to the end of the mourning rite,[415] as if the two professional mourners were shaven at the end of the funerary ceremony as a finalization of the mummy's resurrection. So can we really know what those two women did at the end of the funerals? The most explicit iconography about the end of the funerary ceremony is located in the tomb of Rekhmire. It shows how, after the Opening of the Mouth Ceremony, a woman with short hair is offering green make-up (fig. 36).[416] This was not an arbitrary offering, but very significant, since the make-up was related to the healthy eye of Horus ever since the Old Kingdom: "*the healthy eye of Horus is being made up in your face, two pouches of green make-up*" [417] or "*Horus has made up to you his eye*". [418] Also in the *Coffin Texts* we can find many references of that practice: "*...I make up to you a green eye of Horus in your face*", [419] "*green make-up and black make-up I give you the eye of Horus, black and white...they will lighten your face*". [420] According to these texts, giving make-up is a synonym of giving the Udjat eye.

↑ Fig. 37
Funerals from the tomb of Rekhmire (TT100). In the middle the kneeling mourner offers green make-up. Thebes. Dynasty XVIII (After Davies N., *The Tomb of Rekhmire at Thebes*. New York, 1943)

According to Z. el-Kordy, the offering of make-up was a way of making the full moon come back and to avoid cosmic disorder, so it was a ritual of a lunar nature.[421] In Egyptian funerals it symbolized the victory of Horus over Seth and the offering of the healed eye (Udjat eye) to the deceased, who came back to life like Osiris did in the myth.

On one hand, we have seen that in the Egyptian funerary texts, cutting the *s3mt* was related to the healing of the eye of Horus and to the shaving of the two mourners. On the other hand, the Egyptian iconography shows the offering of make-up (Udjat eye) after the Opening of the Mouth Ceremony, by a mourner without a mane of hair. So it is tempting to think that the cutting of the *s3mt* refers to the shaving of the two *ḏrty* at the end of the revitalizing process in favour of the mummy. According to W.A. Ward, "to cut the *s3mt*" refers to cutting the hair that had grown during the lament and indicated the official end of mourning. In my opinion it would be more precise to say that "*to cut the s3mt*" meant to cut of the professional mourners' hair, which during the mourning rite was manipulated with gestures of a regenerating purpose. At the final moment of that ritual, the hair would be cut off as a symbol of the dead's resurrection. That would explain the

415 Ward, 1975, p.62, n. 17; Borghouts, 1970, p.73.

416 S. Hodel-Hoenes, 1991, p.130

417 *Pyr.*, 54b-55.

418 *Pyr.*, 609.

419 *CT* VII, 936.

420 *CT* VII, 934.

421 Z. el-Kordy, 1982, p.201.

images in the tombs of the New Kingdom of the two *ḏrty* with their hair covered during the funerary procession and without a mane of hair at the end of the funeral. This could also be in agreement with the archaeological remains found in many Egyptian tombs, tentatively identified as hair offerings.[422]

Everything points to an Egyptian funerary custom of shaving or cutting a piece of hair of the two professional mourners in the role of Isis and Nephthys at the end of the mourning rite they carried out during the Opening of the Mouth Ceremony. Cutting this hair meant the official end of the mourning rite, the hair, *smꜣ*, became hair, *sꜣmt*, a symbol of the Udjat eye and therefore a guarantee of the dead's resurrection.

422 *Vide supra* p.12.

PART II | **RESURRECTION**

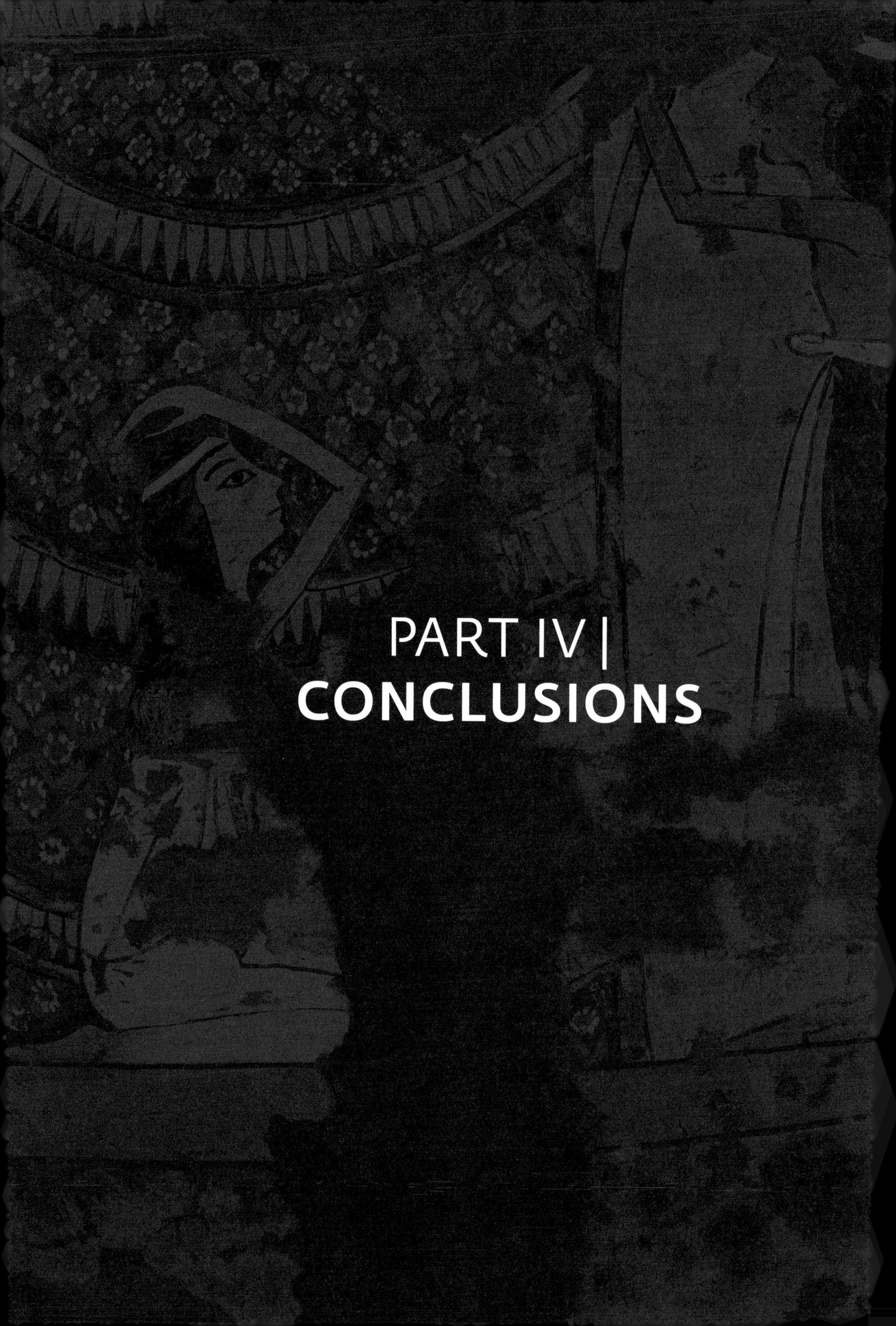

PART IV | CONCLUSIONS

In the course of this work we have seen that hair, in its different aspects, was an essential element in the Egyptian funerary ceremony. Hair was a tool for revival, the handling and symbolism of which assisted in the deceased's resurrection. The hair had two dimensions, ritual and symbolic, depending on how the mourners treated it during the mourning rite and on the strong symbolic meaning of each of the hair swats or elements. Hair, *smꜣ*, the most precise meaning of which seems to be the hair that comes from the crown of the head, was directly related in the funerals to the *nwn* gesture, which had two variations: *nwn* (to shake the hair forwards, covering the face with it) and *nwn m* (to pull the lock of hair *swt/syt*). The *nwn* gesture made with the hair, *smꜣ*, had a very deep dual meaning: symbolic and ritual, and also negative and positive.

1. The symbolic meaning of hair

Hair is darkness

In Ancient Egyptian belief, the hair, *smꜣ*, meant the darkness of death, since the hair over the face prevented the mourners from seeing. With the *nwn* gesture the women reproduced the deceased's blindness. It was also a way of alluding to the dead person's lack of knowledge, because not to see, meant not to know; it was the state of unconsciousness typical of death.

Hair is damage

The negative nature of the *nwn* gesture came not only from the darkness caused by the hair, *smꜣ*, but also from the evil it symbolised. The hair, *smꜣ*, was assimilated to the damage done to the lunar eye. The hair, *smꜣ*, in the Egyptian funerary belief was the image of the disaster that caused the blindness, the evil that Seth caused to the eye of Horus, the lack of moon (and the lack of light) in the night sky. The mourners on earth had their hair over their faces, and in the mythical sphere the lunar eye had no vision and it could not illuminate the night. In order to recover this brightness, it was necessary to eliminate the evil, in the mythic dimension this is when Thoth spat on the *smꜣ* and healed the lunar eye. The night had its natural guide again, the moon, which was fundamental in the entire regenerating process.

Hair is water

The women's hair was also assimilated to water. To offer the hair, *smꜣ*, was a way of offering the primordial waters of the first moment in Egyptian cosmogony. The regenerating rite during funerals was mainly a ceremony of creation, therefore it was necessary to remember the primordial waters (*Nun*) where the world came from. By making the *nwn* gesture of throwing the hair forwards, the mourners transferred the *Nun* to the corpse, the mythical waters from which everything originated. This is a very important step in the regenerating rite, since the restoring waters (the mourner's hair in funerals) erased the mortal past and transported the deceased into a new eternal existence. Coming back to this primeval moment, the dead became an "*inert one in the Nun,*"[423] in a way, this was the same moment as when a mother's water broke and a child was (re)born. And so the dead became a newborn baby.

423 Designation to the corpse in *CT* IV, 334.

Hair, *smꜣ*, also symbolizes the waters of the annual inundation. The *nwn* gesture was also a practice in the Festival of the Valley and the Sed Festival. Both celebrations coincided with the appearance of Sothis in the sky and the following rise of the Nile, and both festivals were a process of death and resurrection for guaranteeing the continuity of, respectively, the god Amun and Pharaoh's power. In both events there was a group of dancers making the *nwn* gesture. By throwing their hair forwards these dancing women they were announcing the regenerating waters, which would renew the power of both god and king. In the mourning rite, the mourners would send the renewing waters to the deceased by shaking their manes of hair.

Hair is vegetation

The connection of hair with nature was not only its association to water. Egyptian funerary literature shows the hair of Isis and Nephthys as an image of both banks of the Nile and, according to Pausanias, the tears dropping from the eyes of Isis were like the water in the riverbed. These two premises converted the two tresses of hair framing the face into the vegetation on each bank of the Nile. In addition, Egyptian language designated a "land with no plants" as a "bald land"; therefore, there was a clear link between hair and vegetation. So, the pieces of hair (associated with vegetation) of the two mourners would be a metaphoric image of the two banks of the river.

The growing of plants is a natural rebirth, so making the *nwn* gesture and throwing the hair assimilated to vegetation could be understood as a way of transferring life to the corpse; in the funerary dimension this would be a way of contributing to the mummy's resurrection.

Hair is maternity

When the mourner made the *nwn* gesture of throwing the hair forwards over her face she turned into the deceased's mother, from whose body he would be reborn. The mummy, assimilated with Osiris, was Nut's son and this goddess was also depicted making the *nwn* gesture inside the coffin, where the regeneration process happened. Nut bent forward and with her hair extended forwards she gave birth to her son Osiris, i.e. the dead. Therefore, inside many coffin lids there was an image of Nut with the arms raised and her hair seemingly standing upright. This is the way in which the artist could represent this goddess on the surface of the coffin lid, although in reality she was thought to bent forwards making the *nwn* gesture.

Additionally, giving the hair, *smꜣ* (*rdi smꜣ*), was a gesture linked to the act of nursing. The mother's milk, which is the first nourishment of a human being, reinforces the Egyptian funerary concept of the dead as a baby. So giving the hair, *smꜣ*, contributed to this idea of the mummy as a newborn baby.

2. The ritual meaning of hair

Hair gives breath

Hair had not just a deep symbolic meaning in Ancient Egypt, it also had a strong ritual connotation. A very important part of the funerals in Ancient Egypt was the Opening of the Mouth Ceremony; a practice that recalled the mythical death and resurrection of Osiris. Among the regenerating rites, there was a mourning ritual executed by two professional mourners incarnating Isis and Nephthys, who assisted the corpse in a symbolic way, recalling the myth through the rite. The legend tells how the goddess Isis, while mourning the death of her husband, became a kite and placed herself above his mummy; flapping her wings she could give the breath of life to Osiris and helped him in his reanimation. In Ancient Egyptian belief, hair and feathers were related, therefore the *nwn* gesture of the mourner shaking the hair, *smꜣ,* towards the corpse could be interpreted as a way of producing the air that the deceased needed for breathing and coming back to life.

Hair signifies sex

By transforming into a kite and placing herself on top of the phallus of Osiris' mummy, Isis could also restore Osiris' virility. According to Egyptian funerary texts, when the mourners gave their hair to the deceased, the deceased impregnated those women. When the mourner was making the *nwn* gesture, she was making a symbolic movement with her hair, *smꜣ,* recalling the episode of the Osiris legend when Isis, on top of the mummy, restored the virility of her husband and copulated with him. The ejaculation of Osiris was a very important step in the myth because it was proof of his physical regeneration. In fact, the virility of the dead was itself a sign of revival and in many representations, to indicate the resurrection of the deceased, he was depicted with "penile erection". It also granted the conception of Horus, Osiris heir and avenger, the one who eliminated the evil and restored order, who succeeded him on the throne of Egypt and who allowed his father to be revived as king of the Hereafter.

The hair, *sꜣmt*, (the Udjat Eye) is cut

sꜣmt is an Egyptian word related to both mourning and hair. And it is closely linked to the idea of the destruction of evil, the healing of the lunar eye and the final recovery of the Udjat eye. The *sꜣmt* could probably be considered as the hair that, during the mourning rite, the two professional mourners moved with a symbolic meaning, shaking it forwards (*nwn smꜣ*) or pulling it (*nwn m swt*). This *sꜣmt* was later cut in order to remove the bad and to recover the Udjat eye as a symbol of the final resurrection. According to the funerary literature, firstly Thoth spat on the damaged eye of Horus, and this action was narrated in sacred texts as "Thoth spitting on the hair, *smꜣ*". Afterwards, the two mourners were shaven, the *sꜣmt* was cut and was offered as the Udjat eye to the deceased. That meant the end of the official mourning rite executed by the two representatives of Isis and Nephthys and the dead's resurrection.

3. Reconstruction of (the funerary) events

Finally I would like to try to place everything we have been looking at inside the funeral ritual of Ancient Egypt. It is just a generic reconstruction, which will help us to sequence the different moments of the mourning ritual and to situate the rites and characters in the funerary ceremony. In the course of this research we have found three different

mourners involved in Egyptian funerals:
In the funerary procession there were groups of common mourners (mainly women, but sometimes also men) among the other members of the procession. They were walking together, weeping and making typical gestures of mourning: beating themselves, raising their arms, ripping their clothes, etc. Those gestures included shaking the hair and covering their face with it (*nwn*) or pulling on a lock of hair (*nwn m*). Egyptian documents (texts and iconography) do not provide evidence that both gestures were made at the same time; common mourners made either one or the other and the group as a whole probably did not make the same gestures at the same time. It seems that there was no coordination in this part of the procession and that the lamenting women could make different mourning movements.

Secondly, the funerary ceremony in Ancient Egypt counted also on the participation of two professional mourners, who played the roles of Isis and Nephthys. They usually appeared at both ends of the coffin in a static way, in contrast to the dynamic depiction of the common mourners. However, funerary texts refer to them as active members in the corpse's regeneration.[424]

If we would reconstruct the puzzle with all the pieces from the different documents the ideal funerary ritual we can now reconstruct is the following: the funerary procession would start at the embalming place, moving towards the necropolis. During the procession the two professional mourners moved static at both ends of the corpse, while the group of common mourners lamented the death crying, screaming and shaking and/or pulling their hair. In this manner, these common mourners symbolized the darkness in which the deceased was, the lack of brightness, the chaos of the primordial waters from which the new life had to come. Once the procession had arrived at the tomb, the scene and rituals changed. We can imagine that the priests and the two mourners went inside the tomb, while the rest of the members of the procession stayed outside.

Inside the tomb the Opening of the Mouth Ceremony for reviving the mummy probably took place. The priestly team entered the mythical dimension here; the myth became a rite and a series of practices for accomplishing the deceased's resurrection was performed here. Ritually, the two professional mourners turned into Isis and Nephthys (the two kites or *ḏrty*) and the mummy turned into Osiris. Inside the tomb the two representatives of Isis and Nephthys carried out the official mourning ritual in which they made the *nwn* and/or the *nwn m* gestures with their hair towards the corpse. This way they reproduced that part of the Osiris myth in which Isis conceived Horus, so he could avenge his father's death. Outside the tomb, the common mourners (including the deceased's wife) kept on moaning.

---

424 Egyptian iconography, especially depictions in tombs and papyri from the New Kingdom, show us the deceased's widow next to the coffin also weeping and making mourning gestures, but apparently never shaking or pulling her hair. She is the mourning wife, but different from the group of common mourners and from the two representatives of Isis and Nephthys.

At some moment during the Opening of the Mouth Ceremony the sacrifice of an ox took place in the presence of the mourners. The animal's slaughter meant the victory of Horus over Seth, good over evil, signalling the end of mourning. At that moment, the mourner's hair, *sꜣmt,* was cut. Cutting this mourner's hair symbolized the enemies' annihilation, the end of the mourning and the *Udjat* eye's recovery. This was done at the end of the Opening of the Mouth Ceremony when, among other things, this form of hair offering took place. It was the mourner's hair that had been shaken and pulled and that served as a symbol of the revitalization process of the mummy (return to the primordial waters and to the mother's womb, recovery of vital powers, etc.) and the removal of the evil, which could prolong that process (lunar eye suffering, enemy, chaos, etc.). This mourner's hair was cut/shaven and offered to the mummy as an image of the *Udjat* eye. This might also explain some archaeological remains mentioned before (especially locks of hair in some tombs). This final act materialised the deceased's resurrection.

The mummy was then put inside the sepulchral chamber, the priests and the two professional mourners left the scene where the resurrection rites had taken place and joined the rest of the funerary retinue that waited outside. The dead's new life had now become a fact.

Bibliography

ALEXIOU, M., *The Ritual Lament in Greek Tradition*. Cambridge, 1974.

ALLAM, Sch., «Beiträge zum Hathorkult (bis zum Ende des Mitteleren Reiches». *MÄS* 4, 1963.

ALLEN, T.G., *The Book of the Dead or Going forth by Day*. Chicago, 1974.

ALLIOT, «Le culte d'Horus à Edfou au temps des Ptolomees». *BdE* XX, 2 vol. Le Caire. 1949-1955.

ALTENMÜLLER, H., «Die Texte zum Begräbnisritual in den Pyramiden des Alten Reiches». ÄA 24, Wiesbaden,1972.

AMMAR, H., *Growing up in an Egyptian Village. (Silwa, Province of Aswan)*. London, 1954.

ARIES, Ph., *L'homme devant la mort*. París, 1977.

ASSMANN, J., «Die Inschrift auf dem äusseren Sarkophagdeckel des Merenptah». *MDAIK*, Band 28. 1972, pp. 47-74.

AWADALLA, A.; Okasha, S., «Une paroi de la tombe du chancelier royal *P3-Nxsy* à Héliopolis». *Orientalia* 58, fasc. 4, 1989, pp. 493-496.

AUFRÈRE, S., *L'Univers minéral dans la pensée égyptienne. BdE* 105. Le Caire, 1991.

AUFRÉRE, S., "Le cosmos, le minéral, le végétal et le divin", *Bulletin du Cercle lyonnais d'égyptologie Victor Loret*, 7, 1993, pp.7-24.

AYROUT, H.H., *Moeurs et coutumes des fellahs*. París, 1938.

BARGUET, P., *Les Textes des Sarcophages du Moyen Empire*. Paris, 1986.

BARGUET, P., *Le Livre des Morts des Anciens Égyptiens. LAPO*, Paris, 1967.

BARGUET, P., «L'Am-Douat et les funérailles royales». *RdE* 24, 1972, pp.7-11.

BARGUET, P., «Le Livre des Cavernes et la reconstitution du corps divin». *RdE* 28, 1976, pp. 25-37.

BARUCQ, A. et DAUMAS, F., *Hymnes et prières de l'Égypte ancienne. LAPO*, Paris, 1980.

BELL, M. R., «Gurob Tomb 605 and Mycenaean Chronology». *Mélanges Gamal Eddin Mokhtar. IFAO*. Le Caire, 1985, pp. 61-86.

BERLEV, O.; BRESCIANI, E.; CAMINOS, R.A.; et allii, *L'homme égyptien*. Paris, 1992.

BERNAND, E., *Inscriptions métriques de l'Égypte gréco-romain*, n° 24. (Chénoboskion IIs. Ap. J-C.). París, 1969.

BLACKMAN, W.S., *Les fellahs de la Haute-Égypte*. París, 1948.

BOAK, A.E.R., "The Organisation of Gilds in Graeco-Roman Egypt". *TAPhA*, 68, 1937.

BONNEAU, D., *La crue du Nil, divinité égyptienne à travers mille ans d'histoire. (332 av.- 641 ap. J.-C.)* París, 1964.

BONNET, H., *Reallexikon der* ágyptischen *Religionsgeschichte*. Berlín, 1952.BORGHOUTS, J.F., *The Magical Texts of Papyrus Leiden I, 348*. OMRO LI, Leiden, 1970.BOURRIAU, J., *Pharaohs and Mortals. Egyptian Art in the Middle Kingdom*. Cambridge, 1988.

BRESCIANI, E., «Éléments de rituel et d'offrande dans le texte démotique». *Ritual and Sacrifice in the Anciente Near East. OLA* 55. Leuven, 1993, pp.45-49.

BRIFFAULT, R., *Las madres. La mujer desde el matriarcado hasta la sociedad moderna*. Buenos Aires, 1974.

BRUNNER-TRAUT, E., *Der Tanz im alten* Ägypten. Glückstadt. 1938

BRUNNER-TRAUT, E., «Die Wochenlaube». *MIO* 3, 1955, pp. 11-72.

de BUCK, A., *The Egyptian Coffin Texts*. Vols. I-VII, Chicago, 1935-1961.

de BUCK, A., «The earliest version of Book of the Dead 78». *JEA* 35. 1949, pp. 87-97.

BUDGE, E. A. WALLIS, *The Gods of the Egyptians*. 2 vols. New York, 1969.

BUDGE, E. A. WALLIS, *Osiris and the Egyptian Resurrection*. New York, 1973.

CASAJUS, D., *La tente dans la solicitude. La société et les morts chez les Tuaregs Kel Ferwan*. París, 1987.

CAUVILLE, S., «Chentayt et Merkhetes, des avatars d'Isis et Neftis». *BIFAO* 81, 1981, pp. 21-40.

CERVELLÓ AUTUORI, J., *Egipto y* África. *Orígen de la civilización y la monarquía faraónicas en su contexto africano*. Barcelona, 1996.

CIRLOT, J. E., *Diccionario de símbolos*. Barcelona, 1991.

CHEVALIER, J. et GHEERBRANDT, A., *Dictionnaire des symboles. Mythes, rêves, coutumes, gestes, formes, figures, couleurs, nombres*, 4 vols., París, 1969.

CLÈRE, J.J., *Les Chauves d'Hathor*. Leuven, 1995.

CROMPTON, W.M., «Two clay Balls in the Manchester Museum». *JEA* 3, 1916, p. 128.DARESSY, M.G., «Les cercueils des prêtres d'Amon. (Deuxième trouvaille de Deir el-Bahari)». *ASAE* VIII. Le Caire, 1907, pp. 3-38.

DAUMAS, F., «La scène de la résurrection au tombeau de Pétosiris». *BIFAO* 59, 1960, pp. 63-80.

DAVIES- GARDINER, *Tomb of Amenemhet*. EEF, 1915.

DECKER, W., *Sport und Spiel im Alten* Ägypten. München, 1987.

DEGARDIN, J.C., «Correspondances osiriennes entre les temples d'Opet et de Khonsu». *JNES*, vol. 44, n° 2, 1985, pp. 115-131.

DELVAUX, L.; Warmenbol, E., *Les divins chats d'Égypte*. Leuven, 1991.

DERCHAIN, Ph., *La lune, mythes et rites. SourOr* 5, París, 1962.

DERCHAIN, Ph., «La pêche de l'oeil et les mystères d'Osiris à Dendera». *RdE* 15, 1963, pp. 11-25.

DERCHAIN, Ph., *Le Papyrus Salt 825 (B.M. 10051). Rituel pour la conservation de la vie en Égypte*. Académie Royale de Belgique, Cl. Lettres, *Mémoires* 58/1a, 1965.

DERCHAIN, Ph., *Hathor quadrifons*. Istanbul, 1972.

DERCHAIN, Ph., «La perruque et le cristal». *SAK* 2, 1975, pp. 55-74.

DERCHAIN-URTEL, M.Th., «Les scènes rituelles des temples d'époque grécoromaine en Égypte et les régles du jeu 'Domino'». *OLA* 55, Leuven, 1993, pp. 99-105.

DERRET, J.D.M., «Religious Hair». *MAN* 8, 1973, pp. 100-103.

DESROCHES-NOBLECOURT, Ch., «Une coutume égyptienne méconue». *BIFAO* 45, 1947, pp. 185-232.

DESROCHES-NOBLECOURT, Ch., «Concubines du mort et mères de famille au Moyen Empire». *BIFAO* 53, 1953, pp. 7-47.

DESROCHES-NOBLECOURT, Ch., «Isis Sothis-le chien, la vigne-, et la tradition millénaire». *MIFAO* 104, 1980, pp. 15-24.

DESROCHES-NOBLECOURT, Ch., *La femme au temps des pharaons*. Paris, 1986.

DONDELINGER, E., *El libro sagrado del Antiguo Egipto. Papiro de Ani, British Museum 10470*. Traducción del alemán por Adela Rodríguez Vargas y Víctor Martínez Lapera. Madrid, 1988.

DRIOTON, E., «Le rôle funéraire d'Hathor au Moyen Empire». *BiOr* 15, 1958, pp. 188-190.

DUNAND, F.; HEIM, J.L.; HENEIN, N.; LICHTENBERG, R., *La nécrpole de Douch (Oasis de Kharga). DFIFAO* 26, 1992.

DURAND, G., *Las estructuras antropológicas de lo imaginario*. Paris, 1979.

DZIOBEK, E.; RAZIQ, M.A., *Das Grab des Sobekhotep. Theben Nr. 63*. Deutsches Archäologisches Institut. Abteilung Kairo. Mainz am Rhein. 1990

DZIOBEK, E., *Das Grab des Ineni. Theben Nr. 81. DAIK*. 1992.

EDWARDS, I.E.S., «Something which Herodotus may have seen». *RdE* 27, 1975, pp. 117-124.

ELIADE, M., *Images et symboles*. Paris, 1952

ELIADE, M., *Traité d'histoire des réligions*. Paris, 1970.

ENEL, *Le mystère de la vie et de la mort d'après l'enseignement des temples de l'ancienne Égypte*.

París, 1985.

EPRON, L.; DAUMAS, F.; MONTET, P., *Le Tombeau de Ti*. Fasc. I. *MIFAO* LXV,1. 1939.

ERMAN, A., «Zauberspruche für Mutter und Kind». *APAW*. 1901, pp. 1-35.

ERMAN, A., *La réligion des égyptiens*. Paris, 1952.

ERMAN, A. und GRAPOW, H., *Wörterbuch der* Ägyptischen *Sprache*. Bände I-V. Berlin, 1982.

ESCHWEILER, P., *Bildzauber im alten* Ägypten. *OBO*, 137

FAKHRY, A., «A note on the Tomb of Kheruef at Thebes». *ASAE* XLII, 1943, pp. 449-508.

FAULKNER, R.O., *The Papyrus Bremner-Rhind. (British Museum No. 10188)*. *BiblAeg*. III. Bruselas, 1933.

FAULKNER, R.O., «The Bremner-Rhind Papyrus-I (A. The Songs of Isis and Nephtys)». *JEA* 22, 1936, pp. 121-140.

FAULKNER, R.O., «The Lamentations of Isis and Nephtys». *MIFAO* 66, 1961, pp.337-348.

FAULKNER, R.O., «The Pregnancy of Isis». *JEA* 54, 1968, pp.40-44.

FAULKNER, R.O., *The Ancient Egyptian Pyramid Texts*. Oxford, 1969.

FAULKNER, R.O., «Coffin Texts Spell 313». *JEA* 58, 1972, pp.91-94.

FAULKNER, R.O., *The Egyptian Coffin Texts*. 3 vols. 1973-1978.

FAULKNER, R.O., *The Ancient Egyptian Book of the Dead*. London, 3ª ed., 1990.

FAULKNER, R,O, *A Concise Dictionary of Middle Egyptian*. Oxford, 1962.

FISCHER, H.G., «Representations of *Dryt*-mourners in the Old Kingdom». *Egyptian Studies* I. Varia. 1976, pp.39-50.

FOX, M.V., «A Study of Antef». *Orientalia*, vol. 46, fasc. 4, 1977, pp.393-423.

FRANCO, I., *Rites et croyances d'éternité*. París, 1993.

FRANKFORT, H., *The Cenotaph of Seti I at Abydos*. *EES*. 1993

FRAZER, J.G., *Adonis, Attis, Osiris. Studies in the History of Oriental Religion*. The Golden Bough. Third Edition. London, 1914.

GABALLA, G.A.; KITCHEN, K.A., «The Festival of Sokar (Tab. I-II)». *Orientalia*, vol. 38, fasc. 1, 1969, pp.1-76.

GARDINER, A.H., *Egyptian Hieratic Texts (Anastasi I and Koller)*. Leipzig, 1911.

GARDINER, A.H. and PEET, T.E., *The Inscriptions of Sinai*. 2 vols. *EES* 45th Memoir. London, 1952-1955.

GARDINER, A.H., «A Unique Funerary Liturgy». *JEA* 41, 1955, pp.9-17.

GARDINER, A.H., «Hymns to Sobk in a Ramesseum Papyrus». *RdE* 11, 1957, pp.43-59.

GARDINER, A.H., *Egyptian Grammar. Being an Introduction to the Study of Hieroglyphs*. Oxford, third ed., 1988.

DE GARIS DAVIES, N., *Five Theban Tombs. (Being those of Mentuherkhepeshef, User, Daga, Nehemaway and Tati)*. Archaelogical Survey of Egypt. London, 1913.

DE GARIS DAVIES, N., *The Tomb of Antefoker, vizier of Sesostris I, and his Wife, Senet (No. 60)*. *EES*. London, 1920.

DE GARIS DAVIES, N., *The Tomb of Nefer-hotep at Thebes*. New York, 1933.

DE GARIS DAVIES, N., *The Tomb of Rekhmi-re at Thebes*. New York, 1973.

GARSTANG, J., *The Third Egyptian Dynasty at Reqâqnah and Bêt Khallâf*. Westminster, 1904.

GAYET, E., *Musée du Louvre. Stèles de la XII Dynastie*. Paris, 1886.

VAN GENNEP, A., *Les Rites de Passage*. París, 1909.

GOEDICKE, H., «The Story of the Herdsman». *CdE* 90, 1970, pp.244-266.

GOEDICKE, H., «Nephtys, the Divorcee". *Hathor* 2, 1990, pp.39-44.

GOFF, B.L., *Symbols of Ancient Egypt in the late Period (Twenty-first Dynasty)*. La Haya, 1979.

GOHARY, J., *Akhenaten's Sed-Festival at Karnak*. London and New York, 1992.

VON GONZENBACH, V., *Untersuchungen zu den knabenweihen im Isiskult der römischen Kaiserzeit*. Bonn, 1957. (resumen en *AEB*, nº 57214, pp.61-62).GOYON, J.C., «Le cérémonial de glorification d'Osiris du Papyrus du Louvre I 3079 (colonnes 110 à 112)». *BIFAO* 65, 1967, pp.89-156.

GOYON, J.C., *Rituels funéraires de l'ancienne Égypte*. *LAPO*, Paris, 1972.

GOYON, J.C., «Textes mythologiques II: les révélations du mystère des quatre boules». *BIFAO* 75, 1975, pp.349-399.

GRAPOW, H., *Religiöse Urkunde* V. Leipzig, 1915.

GRIFFITH, F.Ll.; THOMPSON, H., *The Demotical Magic Papyrus of London and Leiden*. Oxford, 1904.

GUGLIELMI, W., «Lachen und Weinen in Ethik, Kult und Mythos der Ägypter». *CdE*. 109, 1980, pp.69-86.

GUILHOU, N., "Le masque funéraire", Égypte, Afrique et Orient, 5, 1997, pp.26-30.

GUILMANT, F., *Tombeau de Ramses IX*. *MIFAO* XV, Le Caire, 1907.

GUKSCH, H., *Die Gräber des Nacht-Min und des Men-cheper-Ra-seneb. Theben Nr. 87 un 79*. *DAIK*. Mainz am Rhein. 1995.

GUTBUB, A., «Un emprunt aux Textes des Pyramides dans l'hymne à Hathor, dame de l'ivresse». *Mélanges Maspero* I. *MIFAO* LXVI. Le Caire, 1961, pp.31-72.

HALLPICKE, C.R., «Social Hair». *MAN* 4, 1969, pp.256-264.

HANNIG, R., *Grosses Handwörterbuch* Ägyptisch-*Deutsch. (2.800- 950 v. Chr.)*. Mainz, 1995.

HARRASSOWITZ, O., *Lexicon der* Ägyptologie. Wiesbaden, 1975.

HASSAN, F., «Primeval Goddes to Divine King. The Mythogenesis of Power in the Early Egyptian State». *The Followers of Horus*. Studies dedicated to M. Allen Hoffman. Oxford, 1992, pp.307-322.

HASSAN, S., *Excavations at Gizah. The Mastabas of the Sixth Season and their Description*. Vol. VI, part. III. Cairo, 1934-1935.

HAYES, W.C., *The Burial Chamber of the Trasures Sobk-Mose from Er Rizeikat*. New York, 1939.

HAYS, H. M., «The End of Rites of Passage and a Start with Ritual Syntax in Ancient Egypt», *RSO*. Vol. LXXXVI, Sup. 2, Roma, 2013, pp. 165-186.

HELCK, W., «Nilhöhe und Jubiläumsfest». *ZÄS* 93, 1966, pp.74-79.

HELCK, W., *Die Prophezeiung des Nfrty*. Wiesbaden, 1970.

HELCK, W., *Urkunden der 18. Dynastie. Hefte 20-21*. Berlín, 1984.

HERSHMAN, P., «Hair, Sex and Dirt». *MAN* 9, 1974, pp.274-298.

HODEL-HOENES, S., *Leben und Tod im Alten* Ägypten. *Thebanische Privatgräber des Neuen Reiches*. Darmstadt, 1991.

HORNUNG, E.; STAEHELIN, E., «Studien zum Sedfest». *AH* 1, 1974.

HORNUNG, E., «Das Buch der Anbetung des Re im Westen (Sonnenlitanei)». *AH* 2, 1975; 3, 1976.

DE HORRACK, «Le Livre des Respirations». *BiblÉg* XVII, 1907, p.113.

JANSEN, W., «Zu den Trauerriten bei der Apisbestattung». *BSEG* 18, 1994, pp.33-39.

JOURET, R-M., *Thèbes, 1250 av. J-C. Ramsès II et le rêve du pouvoir absolu*. Autrement, série Mémoires, nº 2, octobre, 1990.

JUNKER, H., *Die Stundenwachen in den Osirismysterien; nach den Inschriften von Dendera, Edu und Philae*. Wien, 1910.

JUNKER, H., *Der Auszug der Hathor-Tefnut aus Nubien*. Berlin, 1911.

JUNKER, H., *Die Onuris-Legende*. Wien, 1917.

JUNKER, H., *Giza*. Vols. I-IX. Wien/Leipzig, 1934.

KAPLONY, P., *Kleine Beiträge zu den Inschriften der* Ägyptischen *Frühzeit*. Wiesbaden, 1966.

KEEL, O., *Die Weisheit Spielt vor Gott*. Freiburg und Gottingen, 1974.

KEES, «Zu den ägyptischen Mondsagen». *ZÄS* 60, 1925, pp.1-16.

KEES, *Totenglauben und Jenseitsvorstellungen der alten* Ägypter. Berlin, 1956.

KITCHEN, K.A., *Rameside Inscriptions. Historical and Biographical.* VI, Oxford, 1969.

EL-KORDY, Z., «L'offrande des fards dans les temples ptolemaïques». *ASAE* LXVIII. 1982, pp.195-222.

KOROSTOVTSEV, M., «Stèle de Ramsès IV». *BIFAO* 45. 1947, pp.155-173.

KRISTENSEN, W.B., *Life out of Death.* Louvain, 1992.

LACAU, P., *Sarcophages antérieurs au Nouvel Empire*. Cairo *CGC*. 1903-1904.

LACAU, P., *Textes religieux égyptiens*. Première partie. Paris, 1910.

LEFEBURE, E., *Les hypogeés royaux de Thèbes*. Vol. I, II, III. *MMAF*. Paris, 1886.

LEFEBURE, E., «Étude sur Abydos. III. Un dialogue des morts: le chapitre d'amener la barque». Ouvres Diverses. *BiblÉg* II, Paris, 1912, pp.287-306.

LEFEBURE, G., *Le tombeau de Petosiris*. 3 vols. Le Caire, 1923-1924.

LEFEBVRE, G., *Romans et contes égyptiens de l'époque pharaonique*. Paris, 1988.

LEFEBVRE, G., *Grammaire de l'égyptien classique*, deuxième ed., *IFAO*, Le Caire, 1990.LEPSIUS, C.R., *Denkmäler aus* Ägypten *und* Äthiopien. Genève, 1972.

LE QUELLEC, J-L., *Symbolisme et art rupestre au Sahara*. Paris, 1993.

LICHTHEIM, M., *Ancient Egyptian Literature: a Book of Readings*. Vol. I, *The Old and the Middle Kingdoms,* Berkeley, 1973.

LICHTHEIM, M., *Ancient Egyptian Literature. A Book of Readings.* Vol. II, *The New Kingdom*, Berkeley, 1976.

LICHTHEIM, M. *Ancient Egyptian Literature: a Book of Readings.* Vol.III, *The Late Period,* Berkeley, 1980.

LODS, A., *Israël, des origines au milieu du VIII siècle*. Paris, 1930.

LOPES, M.H.T., «O mito de Osiris: analise de un mito fundador». *HATHOR* 2, 1990, pp.7-16.

LÓPEZ, J., «Mitología y religión egipcias». *Mitología y religión del Antiguo Oriente I. Egipto y Mesopotamia*. Barcelona, 1993.

LÜDDECKENS, E., «Untersuchungen über religiösen Gehalt, Sprache und Form der ägyptischen Totenklagen». *MDAIK* 11, 1943.

LULL, J. *La astronomía en el antiguo Egipto*. Valencia, 2006.

LURKER, M., *Götter und Symbole der Alten* Ägypter. München, 1974.

MANNICHE, L., *Lost Tombs. A Study of certain Eighteenth Dynasty Monuments in the Theban Necropolis*. London- New York. 1988.

MARIETTE, A., *Dendérah. Description générale du grand temple de cette ville.* Vols. I-IV. Le Caire, 1875.

MARIETTE, A., *Abydos* II. Paris, 1880.

MASPERO, M., *Trois années de fouilles dans les tombeaux de Thèbes et de Memphis*. *MMAF*. Tome I, fasc. 2. Le Caire, 1885.

MASPERO, G., «Études de mythologie et d'archéologie égyptiennes». *BiblÉg*. I-VI. París, 1893-1912.

MATHIEU, B., «Les hommes des larmes. À propos d'un jeu de mots mythique dans les textes de l'ancienne Égypte». *Hommages à François Daumas*. Montpellier, 1986, pp.499-509.

MAYASSIS, S., *Le Livre des Morts de l'Égypte Ancienne est un livre d'initiation*. Athènes, 1955.

MAYASSIS, S., *Mystères et initiations de l'Égypte Ancienne*. Athènes. 1957.

MBITI, J.S., *African Religions and Philosophy*. Second Edition. 1990.

MEEKS, D., «Notes de lexicographie». *RdE* 28, 1976, pp.87-96.

MEEKS, D., *Année Lexicographique, Égypte ancienne*. Vols. I-III. Paris, 1977-1979.MEEKS, D., «Dieu masqué, dieu sans tête». *Archéo-Nil* 1, 1991, pp.5-15.

MICHALOWSKI, K., *Arte y civilización de Egipto*. Paris, 1969.

MICHALOWSKI, K., *Karnak*. München, 1970.

MONTET, P., *La necropole royal de Tanis.* Tome III (Chéchanq III). París, 1955.

MORET, A., *Mystères égyptiens*. Paris, 1913.

MORET, A., *La mise à mort du dieu en Égypte*. Paris, 1927.

MORET, A., «Légende d'Osiris à l›époque thébaine d›après l›hymne à Osiris du Louvre». *BIFAO* 30, 1931, pp.725-750.

MUELLER, D., «An early Egyptian Guide to the Hereafter». *JEA* 58, 1972. pp.99-125.

MÜLLER, M., *Mitología egicia*. Barclona, 1996.

MÜNSTER, M., «Untersuchungen zur Göttin Isis vom Alten Reich bis zum Ende des Neuen Reiches». *MÄS* 11, 1968.

NACTERGAEL, G., «Bérénice II, Arsinoé III et l'offrande de la boucle». *CdE* LV, 109-110, 1980, pp.240-253.

NAGUIB, S., *Le clergé féminin d'Amon thébain à la 21 Dynastie*. *OLA* 38. Leuven, 1990.

NAGUIB, S., «Hair in Ancient Egypt». *AcOr (K)* 51, 1990, pp.7-26.

NAGUIB, S., «Miroirs du Passé». *CSEG*. Vol. II, Genève, 1993.

NAVILLE, E., *La litanie du soleil. Inscriptions recueillies dans les tombeaux des rois à Thèbes*. Leipzig, 1875.

NAVILLE, E., *The Festival-Hall of Osorkon II in the Great Temple of Bubastis*. *EEF*. London, 1892.

NAVILLE, E., *Das* Ägyptishe *Totenbuch der XVIII bis XX Dynastie*. Band I. Text und Vignetten. Wien. 1971.

NEVEU, F., *La langue des Ramsès. Grammaire du Néo-égyptien*. Paris, 1996.

OSING, J., «Isis und Osiris». *MDAIK* 30, 1974, pp.91-114.

OSING, J., *Das Grab des Nefersecheru in Zawyet Sultan*. Mainz am Rhein, 1992.

OTTO, E., «An Ancient Egyptian Hunting Ritual». *JNES* 9, 1950, pp.164-177.

OTTO, E., «Das ägyptische Mundöffnungsritual». ÄA 3, Wiesbaden, 1960.

PEET, T.E., «A remarkable Burial Custom of the Old Kingdom». *JEA* 2, 1915, pp.8-9.

PEET, T.E.; Woolley, C.L., *The City of Akhenaten. I. EES*. London, 1923.

PETRIE, W.M.F., *Deshasheh*. London, 1898.

PETRIE, W.M.F., *Abydos*. Part I. London, 1902.

PIANKOFF, A., «Le Livre des Quererts. 1° Tableau». *BIFAO* 41. 1942, pp.1-11.

PIANKOFF, A., «Le Livre des Quererts. Seconde Division». *BIFAO* 42, 1944, pp.1-62.

PIANKOFF, A., «Le Livre des Quererts. Sixième Division (Fin du «Livre des Quererts»)». *BIFAO* 43, 1945, pp.1-50.

PIANKOFF, A., *The Litany of Re*. *ERT*. Vol. 4, 1964.

PIANKOFF, A.; Jacquet-Gordon, H., *The Wandering of the Soul*. *ERT*. Vol. 6, 1974.

PORTER, B.; MOSS, R., *Topographical Bibliography of Ancient Egyptian Hieroglyphic Texts, Reliefs and Paintings*. Vols. I-VII. Oxford, 1960.

POSENER, G., «La légende de la tresse d'Hathor». *Egyptological Studies in honor of R. A. Parker*. Hannover-London. 1986, pp.111-117.

QUACK, J.F., «Das Pavianshaar und die Taten des Thot». *SAK* 23, 1996, pp.305-334.

RADWAN, A., «Der Taruergestus als Datierungsmittel». *MDAIK* 30, 1974, pp.115-130.

RANSOM WILLIAMS, C., *The Decoration of the tomb of Per-Neb. The Technique and the Color Conventions*. New York, 1932.

RATIÉ, S., «Quelques réflexions sur l'aspect de l'oeil et sur ses transpositions dans l'ancienne

Égypte». *Mélanges Gutbub*. Montpellier, 1984, pp.177-182.

ROEDER, G., *Mythen und Legenden um* Ägyptische *Gottheiten und Pharaonen*. Ägyptische Religion II. Zürich, 1960.

ROQUET, G., «Chronologie relative des changements phonétiques». *Hommages à Serge Sauneron. BdE* 2 Vols. Le Caire, 1979.

ROSSI, G., *El influjo de la luna en los cultivos*. Barcelona, 1990.

ROTH, A.M., «The *pss-kf* and the 'Opening of the Mouth' Ceremony: A Ritual of Birth and Rebirth». *JEA* 78, 1992, pp.113-147.

ROTH, A.M., «Fingers, Stars and the 'Opening of the Mouth'». *JEA* 79, 1993, pp.57-79.

ROWE, A., «Inscriptions on the Model Coffin containing the lock of hair of Queen Tyi». *ASAE* XL, 1941, pp.623-627.

RUSCH, A., «Ein Osirisritual in den Pyramidentexten». *ZÄS* 60, 1925, pp.16-39.

SÄVE-SÖDERBERGH, T., *Four Eighteenth Dynasty Tombs. (Private Tombs at Thebes)*. Vol. I. Oxford, 1957.

EL-SAYED, R., «Mots et expressions évoquant l'idée de lumière». *ASAE* LXX, 1987, pp.61-86.

SCHÄFER, H., «Die Mysterien des Osiris in Abydos unter König Sesostris III». *UGAÄ*. Band IV. Hildesheim, 1964.

SCHENKEL, W., «Die Gräber des *P3-tnf-i* und eines Unbekanten in der thebanischen Nekropole (Nr. 128 und 129)». *MDAIK* 31, 1975, pp.127-158.

SCHERZ, A.; SCHERZ, E.R., Taapopi, G., et alii, *Hair-styles, head-dresses and ornaments in Namibia and Southern Angola*. Namibia, 1981.

SCHOTT, S., *Altägyptische Festdaten*. Mainz am Rhein, 1950.

SCHOTT, S., *Das schöne Fest vom Wüstentale*. Wiesbaden, 1952.

SETHE, K., *Die altägyptischen Pyramidentexte*. Bände I-IV. Leipzig, 1910.

SETHE, K., *Dramatische Texte zu altägyptischen Mysterienspielen*. Leipzig, 1928.

SETHE, K.; FIRCHOW, O., *Thebanische Tempelinschriften aus griechisch-römischer Zeit*. Urkunden VIII. Berlin, 1957.

SETTGAST, J., *Untersuchungen zu altägyptischen Bestattungsdarstellungen*. Glückstadt. 1963.

SIGRID HOEDEL, H., *Leben und Tod im Alten* Ägypten. Stuttgart, 1991.

SIMPSON, W.K., *The Mastabas of Qar and Idu G. 7101 and G. 7102*. Boston, 1976.

SMITH, W.S., *A History of Egyptian Sculpture and Painting in the Old Kingdom*. Boston, 1946.

SPIELBERG, W., «Varia». *ZÄS* 53, 1917. pp.91-115.

STADELMANN, R., «Les grandes fêtes de Thèbes», *Thèbes 1250 av.J.C. Ramsès II et le rêve du pouvoir absolu*. Autrement; série Mémoires, nº 2, Octobre, 1990, pp.140-153.

STAEHELIN, E., «Bindung und Entbindung». *ZÄS* 96, 1970, pp.125-139.

STAEHELIN, E., «Zur Hathorsymbolik in der ägyptischen Kleinkunst». *ZÄS* 105, 1978, pp.76-84.

TASSIE, G.J., "Hair-Offerings: An Enigmatic Egyptian Custom". *Papers from the Institute of Archaeology*. Vol. 7, 1996, pp.59-67.

TAYLOR, J.J.; GRIFFITH, F.Ll., *The Tomb of Paheri at el-Kab. EEF*. London, 1894.

TEFNIN, R., *Art et magie au temps des pyramides. L'énigme des têtes dites «de remplacement»*. Monumenta Aegyptiaca 5. Bruxelles, 1991.

THOMAS, L.V., *Anthropologie de la mort*. Paris, 1975.

VANDIER, J., *Manuel d'archéologie égyptienne*. Tome IV, París, 1964.

VANDIER, J., *Le Papyrus Jumilhac*. Paris, 1961.

VERCOUTTER, J., *Textes biographiques du Sèrapeum de Memphis*. paris, 1962.

VIREY, Ph., *Le tombeau de Rechmara. MMAF*. Tome V, 1891.

WAGNER, G., «The Abaluyia of Kavirondo (Kenya)». *African Worlds. Studies in the Cosmological Ideas and Social Values of African Peoples*. Oxford, 1954.

WAGNER, G.; BARAKAT, H., DUNAND, F., et allii, «Douch- Rapport préliminaire de la campagne de fouille 1982». *ASAE* LXX, 1984-1985.

WAINWRIGTH, G.A., *Balabish. EES*. London, 1920.

WARD, W. A., «The Biconsonantal Root *b3* and Remarks on Bilabial Interchange in Egyptian». *ZÄS* 102, 1975, pp.60-67.

WERBROUCK, M., *Les pleureuses dans l'Égypte Ancienne*. Bruxelles, 1938.

WHITNEY, M.D., «The Ascension Myth in the Pyramid Texts». *JNES* 36, nº 3, 1977, pp.161-180.

WILD, H., *Le Tombeau de Ti. (La Chapelle)*. Fasc. II. *MIFAO* LXV, 23. Le Caire, 1953.

WILD, H., «Les danses sacrées de l'Égypte Ancienne». *Les Danses Sacrées. SourOr* 6. París, 1963.

WILLEMS, H., "The Coffin of Heqata (Cairo JdE 36418). A Case Study of Egyptian Funerary Culture of the Early Middle Kingdom". *OLA* 70. Leuven, 1996.

WILSON, J.A., «Funeral Services of the Egyptian Old Kingdom». *JNES* 3, 1944, pp.201-218.

WILSON, M., *Communal Rituals of the Nyakyusa*. Oxford, 1959.

WINLOCK, H.E., *The Tomb of Queen Meryet-Amun at Thebes*. New York, 1932.

WINTER, E.H., «La religion des Ambas», en: Middleton, J., *Anthropologie religieuse. Les dieux et les rites (textes fundamentaux)*. 1967.

WYCICHL, W., «La femme aux cheveux d'or». *Société d'Égyptologie de Genève* 1, 1979, p.14.

YOYOTTE, J., «Une étude sur l'anthroponyme gréco-égyptienne du nome prosôpite». *BIFAO* 55, 1956, pp.125-140.

ZANDEE, J., «Book of the Dead, Chapter 83». *BiOr* X, 1953, pp.109-116.

Classical Authors

HERODOTO, *Los Nueve Libros de la Historia*. Ed. Lumen. Traducción de Mª Rosa Lida. Barcelona, 1981.

PLINIO EL VIEJO, *Natural History*. Loeb. Classical Library. London, 1969.

PLUTARCO, *De Iside et Osiride*. University of Wales Press, 1970.

Index

Acknowledgements

On a personal note, I sincerely would like to thank:

Dr. Nadine Guilhou of the Université Paul Valéry of Montpellier, who guided me from the beginning until the end in my research. Also to Dr. Sydney Hervé Aufrère, who accepted me in the Institut d'Égyptology François Daumas, and all the staff there who helped me during my stay.

Dr. Campbell (Curator of Egypt and the Sudan in Manchester Museum, The University of Manchester), Thierry Benderitter (Webmaster of www.osirisnet.net) and the Rijksmuseum of Leiden for allowing me to use their images FOC in this manuscript. I thank also the Metropolitan Museum of Art of New York for having a big archive of images of PUBLIC DOMAIN, allowing their use FOC. To all of them thank you for helping to make culture accessible to the general public.

Printed by Printforce, United Kingdom